FORTY-NINE

ARENAL & MONTEVERDE

CHRISTOPHER P. BAKER

Contents

Arenal & Monteverde

The Northern Zone

Look for ★ to find recommended sights, activities, dining, and lodging.

Highlights

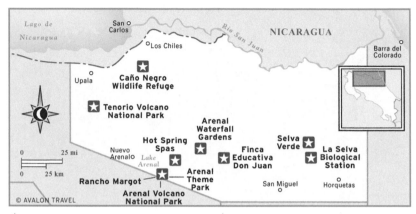

★ **Finca Educativa Don Juan:** Experience a fun and inspiring introduction to organic farming at this family-run farm (page 16).

★ **Hot Spring Spas:** At Balneario Tabacón, one of the enticing hot springs options, you can bathe in steaming waters that tumble from the Volcán Arenal and cascade through a landscaped garden (page 19).

★ **Arenal Waterfall Gardens:** This fantastic set of landscaped hot-springs cascades (and the setting for an episode of *The Bachelor*) also features a wildcat center (page 20).

★ **Arenal Volcano National Park:** With a symmetrical volcano at its heart, this national park has hiking trails over still-warm lava flows and open spaces for prime wildlife-viewing (page 26).

★ **Rancho Margot:** This ecologically self-sustaining farm and wildlife rescue center has rustic but endearing accommodations, plus hiking, rappelling, and horseback riding (page 32).

★ **Arenal Theme Park:** The aerial tram at this private reserve promises high-mountain rides and staggering vistas. Nature trails and canopy tours provide close-up encounters with wildlife (page 32).

★ **Caño Negro Wildlife Refuge:** This croc-infested swamp and forest ecosystem is a dream for bird-watchers, wildlife lovers, and anglers, who hook tarpon, garfish, and snook (page 38).

★ **Tenorio Volcano National Park:** Long off the tourist charts, this volcano is a newfound frontier for hikers. Trail destinations include the jade-colored Río Celeste (page 41).

★ **Selva Verde:** Enfolded by rainforest, this dedicated nature lodge offers instant access to wildlife-rich terrain. Options include guided hikes by day and night, plus canoeing on the Río Sarapiquí (page 46).

★ **La Selva Biological Station:** The wildlife viewing at this scientific research station is awesome. Expect to see peccaries close up on guided walks through the rainforest (page 49).

The northern lowlands constitute a 40,000-square-kilometer (15,400-square-mile) watershed drained by the Ríos Frío, San Carlos, and Sarapiquí and their tributaries, which flow north to the Río San Juan, forming the border with Nicaragua. The rivers meander like restless snakes and flood in the wet season, when much of the landscape is transformed into swampy marshlands. The region is made up of two separate plains (*llanuras*): in the west, the Llanura de los Guatusos, and farther east, the Llanura de San Carlos. Today, travelers are flocking here thanks to the singular popularity of Volcán Arenal and the fistful of adventures based around nearby La Fortuna.

These plains were once rampant with tropical rainforest. During recent decades much of it has been felled as the lowlands have been transformed into farmland. But there's still plenty of rainforest extending for miles across the plains and clambering up the north-facing slopes of the cordilleras, whose scarp face hems the lowlands.

Today, the region is a breadbasket for the nation, and most of the working population is employed in agriculture. The land in the southern uplands area of San Carlos, centered on the regional capital of Ciudad Quesada, is almost 70 percent dedicated to dairy cattle. The lowlands are the realm of beef cattle and plantations of pineapples, bananas, and citrus.

The climate has much in common with the Caribbean coast: warm, humid, and consistently wet. Temperatures hover at 25-27°C (77-81°F) year-round. The climatic periods are not as well defined as those of other parts of the nation, and rarely does a week pass without a prolonged and heavy rain shower (it rains a little less from February to the beginning of May). Precipitation tends to diminish and the dry season grows more pronounced northward and westward.

PLANNING YOUR TIME

Allocate up to one week if you want to fully explore the lowlands. The region is a vast triangle, broad to the east and narrowing to the west. Much of the region is accessible only along rough dirt roads that turn to muddy

Previous: Arenal Volcano; coatimundi at Lake Arenal. **Above:** hikers at La Selva Biological Station.

The Northern Zone

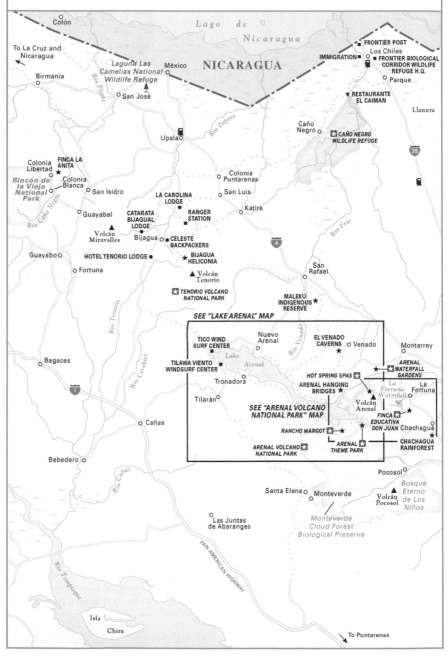

Colón

Lago de Nicaragua

To La Cruz and Nicaragua

Birmania

Laguna Las Camelias National Wildlife Refuge

México

San José

Río Pizote

NICARAGUA

Río Zapote

Upala

FRONTIER POST
Los Chiles
IMMIGRATION ■ ○ ■ FRONTIER BIOLOGICAL CORRIDOR WILDLIFE REFUGE H.Q.
Parque

▼ RESTAURANTE EL CAIMAN

Llanura

35

Caño Negro ○ ☒ CAÑO NEGRO WILDLIFE REFUGE

Colonia Libertad
FINCA LA ANITA ★
Rincón de la Vieja National Park
Colonia Blanca
San Isidro

Guayabal

Colonia Puntarenas

San Luis

Río Caño Negro

LA CAROLINA LODGE

CATARATA BIJAGUAL LODGE
Volcán Miravalles ▲
Bijagua ○ ● CELESTE BACKPACKERS

RANGER STATION

Katira

Río Frío

Guayabo ○

HOTEL TENORIO LODGE ●

Fortuna

BIJAGUA HELICONIA

▲ Volcán Tenorio

San Rafael

☒ TENORIO VOLCANO NATIONAL PARK

4

MALEKÚ INDIGENOUS ★ RESERVE

SEE "LAKE ARENAL" MAP

Río Tenorio

Bagaces

Río Corobicí

TICO WIND SURF CENTER ★

Nuevo Arenal

Lake

TILAWA VIENTO WINDSURF CENTER ■

Tronadora ○

Tilarán ○

Río Venado

Arenal

EL VENADO CAVERNS ○ Venado
★

Monterrey

ARENAL WATERFALL GARDENS

HOT SPRING SPAS ☒

ARENAL HANGING BRIDGES ★

La Fortuna Waterfall ○

La Fortuna

SEE "ARENAL VOLCANO NATIONAL PARK" MAP

Volcán Arenal

FINCA ☒ EDUCATIVA DON JUAN ★

Chachagua

Cañas ○

RANCHO MARGOT ☒ ★

ARENAL ☒ THEME PARK

CHACHAGUA RAINFOREST ★

ARENAL VOLCANO ☒ NATIONAL PARK

Bebedero ○

Río Cañas

1

Pocosol ○

Santa Elena ○ Monteverde

Volcán Pocosol ▲

Bosque Eterno de Los Niños

Las Juntas de Abaranges

Monteverde Cloud Forest Biological Preserve

PAN-AMERICAN HIGHWAY

Río Tempisque

Isla Chira

To Puntarenas

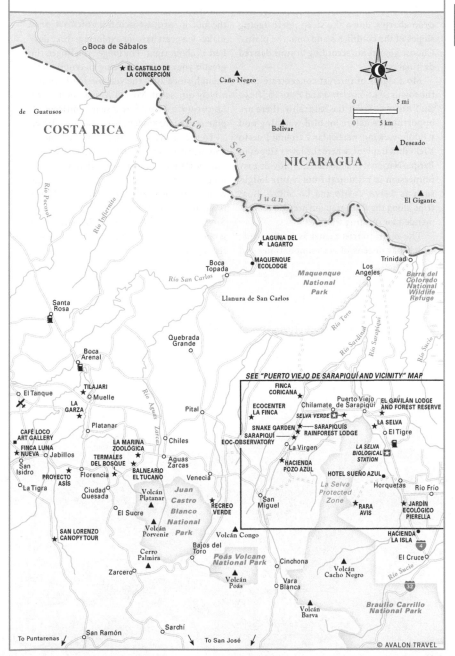

© AVALON TRAVEL

quagmires in the wet season; a 4WD vehicle is essential. You can descend from the Central Highlands via any of half a dozen routes that drop sharply down the steep north-facing slopes of the cordilleras and onto the plains. Choose your route according to your desired destination.

Most sights of interest concentrate near the towns of **La Fortuna** and **Puerto Viejo de Sarapiquí**. For the naturalist, there are opportunities galore for bird-watching and wildlife-viewing, particularly around Puerto Viejo de Sarapiquí, where the lower slopes of Parque Nacional Braulio Carrillo provide easy immersion in rainforest from nature lodges such as **Selva Verde** and **La Selva**. Boat trips along the Río Sarapiquí are also recommended for spotting wildlife.

The main tourist center is La Fortuna, which has dozens of accommodations and restaurants, plus tour companies offering horseback riding, river trips, bicycle rides, and other adventure excursions. Its location at the foot of **Parque Nacional Volcán Arenal** makes it a great base for exploring; three days here is about right. The longer you linger, the greater your chance of seeing an eruption, although since 2010 the volcano has been relatively quiescent. Volcán Arenal looms over **Laguna de Arenal,** whose magnificent alpine setting makes for an outstanding drive.

To the far west, the slopes of the Tenorio and Miravalles volcanoes are less developed but worthwhile, with several new nature lodges around **Bijagua,** one of my favorite regions. To the north, the town of Los Chiles is a gateway to **Refugio Nacional de Vida Silvestre Caño Negro,** a wildlife refuge that is one of the nation's prime bird-watching and fishing sites.

Citrus plantations dominate much of the northern lowlands.

Ciudad Quesada and Vicinity

CIUDAD QUESADA

Ciudad Quesada (pop. 30,000), known locally as San Carlos, hovers above the plains at 650 meters (2,130 feet) elevation on the north-facing slope of the Cordillera de Tilarán, with the lowlands spread out at its feet. Despite its mountainside position, the bustling market town is the gateway to the northern region. It is surrounded by lush pasture grazed by prize-specimen dairy cattle.

The annual Feria del Ganado (Cattle Fair) in April is one of the largest in the country, with a horse parade (*tope*) and general merriment.

Termales del Bosque (tel. 506/2460-4740, www.termalesdelbosque.com, 8am-5pm daily, adults $22, children $12), about five kilometers (3 miles) east of Ciudad Quesada, is billed as an ecological park with hiking trails through botanical gardens, plus horseback rides ($15-45) and mineral hot springs (adults $12, children $6). It offers aromatherapy, mud applications, massages, and hikes into Parque Nacional Juan Castro Blanco.

Juan Castro Blanco National Park

Rising to the southeast of Ciudad Quesada are the still active Volcán Platanar (2,183 meters/7,162 feet) and Volcán Porvenir (2,267 meters/7,438 feet), at the heart of Parque Nacional Juan Castro Blanco. Covering 14,453 hectares (35,714 acres), it protects slopes extending from 700 meters elevation. It is replete with wildlife, including Baird's tapir and, at upper elevations, the resplendent quetzal. It can also be accessed from Bajos del Toro and El Silencio de Los Ángeles Cloud Forest Reserve, in the Central Highlands. The main access is now from El Sucre, about five kilometers (3 miles) south of Ciudad Quesada. A dirt road leads 10 kilometers (6 miles) to a new visitors center (tel. 506/8815-7094, apanajuca@gmail.com, daily 8am-4pm, by donation), from where trails lead through montane rainforest to sparkling lakes.

Restaurante El Congo (tel. 506/8872-9808, 9am-5pm Sat.-Sun.), one kilometer (0.6 miles) before the visitors center, caters to hikers with fresh-caught trout and *comida típica*.

La Marina Zoológica

Private zoo La Marina Zoológica (tel./fax 506/2474-2100, www.zoocostarica.com, 8am-4pm daily, adults $10, children $8), 12 kilometers (7.5 miles) east of Ciudad Quesada, beyond Termales del Bosque on the road to Aguas Zarcas (15 kilometers/9.5 miles east of Ciudad Quesada), houses jaguars, tapirs, agoutis, peccaries, badgers, monkeys, and other mammal species as well as birds from around the world. The Alfaro family has been taking in orphaned animals for three decades, and the zoo now has more than 450 species of birds and other animals, many confiscated by the government from owners who lacked permits to keep them. The zoo even has two lions and successfully breeds tapirs. The zoo is a nonprofit, and donations are appreciated.

Proyecto Asis

Animals lovers will likewise find pleasure at Proyecto Asis (tel. 506/2475-9121, www.institutoasis.com, adults $29, children $17), an animal rescue center at Florencia, about 20 kilometers (13 miles) northwest of Ciudad Quesada. It rehabilitates injured animals, but also serves to educate locates in the conservation ethic. You can even volunteer here.

Accommodations

There's no shortage of budget accommodations in town, most offering a choice of shared or private baths for around $10 pp. Favored by business travelers, Hotel Don Goyo (Calle 2, Ave. 4, tel. 506/2460-1780, $22 s, $33 d) offers 21 clean, modern rooms that stair-step down a hillside. Each has cable TV and a private bath

Ciudad Quesada

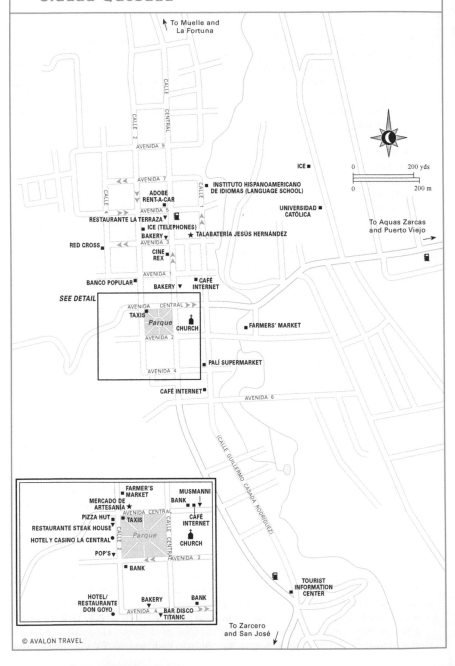

To Muelle and
La Fortuna

CALLE
CALLE 2
CALLE CENTRAL

AVENIDA 9

ICE ■

0   200 yds
0   200 m

AVENIDA 7

CALLE 1

■ INSTITUTO HISPANOAMERICANO
DE IDIOMAS (LANGUAGE SCHOOL)

ADOBE
RENT-A-CAR ■

UNIVERSIDAD ■
CATÓLICA

CALLE 4

AVENIDA 5

RESTAURANTE LA TERRAZA ▼

To Aquas Zarcas
and Puerto Viejo

■ ICE (TELEPHONES)
BAKERY ▼   ★ TALABATERÍA JESÚS HERNÁNDEZ

RED CROSS ■

AVENIDA 3

CINE ■
REX

AVENIDA 1

BANCO POPULAR ■   ■ CAFÉ
BAKERY ▼   INTERNET

SEE DETAIL

AVENIDA   CENTRAL

TAXIS ■

Parque   ✝
CHURCH

AVENIDA 2

■ FARMERS' MARKET

AVENIDA 4

■ PALÍ SUPERMARKET

CAFÉ INTERNET ■

AVENIDA 6

(CALLE GUILLERMO CASADA RODRÍGUEZ)

FARMER'S
■ MARKET

MUSMANNI
BANK

MERCADO DE
ARTESANÍA ★

AVENIDA CENTRAL

■ ■

PIZZA HUT ▼   TAXIS ■

CAFÉ
INTERNET

RESTAURANTE STEAK HOUSE ▼

CALLE 2

✝
CHURCH

HOTEL Y CASINO LA CENTRAL ●

Parque

CALLE CENTRAL

POP'S ▼

AVENIDA 2

■ BANK

HOTEL/
RESTAURANTE
DON GOYO ●

BAKERY
■

BANK
■

AVENIDA 4   BAR DISCO
▼ TITANIC

■ ■
TOURIST
INFORMATION
CENTER

To Zarcero
and San José

© AVALON TRAVEL

with hot water; most have heaps of light. It has a pleasant restaurant.

The more upscale and nature-focused **Termales del Bosque** (tel. 506/2460-4740, www.termalesdelbosque.com, from $70 s, $95 d), on the road to Aguas Zarcas, has 44 attractive, albeit small, modern air-conditioned cabins and four deluxe bungalows amid landscaped grounds in an ecological park with hot springs. Rates include breakfast.

At **Hotel El Tucano Resort & Thermal Spa** (tel. 506/2460-6000, www.hoteltucano. com, from $110 s/d year-round), healing hot springs hiccup out of clefts in the rocks on which the hotel is built. Located eight kilometers (5 miles) east of Ciudad Quesada, the riverside hotel with a large open-air swimming pool is styled loosely as a Swiss chalet complex, with wrought-iron lanterns and window boxes. The 87 guest rooms are rather ho-hum in decor, despite beautiful hardwoods and king beds; master suites are wood-paneled. It has a restaurant, a casino, a full-service spa, forest trails, a gym, tennis, miniature golf, and horseback riding.

Food

The clean and modern **Restaurante Steak House Coca Loca** (tel. 506/2460-3208, 11am-11pm daily, $5-11), on the west side of the plaza, specializes in delicious *lomitos* (steaks), served with pickled jalapeños and black bean sauce.

For ambience head to **La Terraza** (Calle Central, Ave. 3, tel. 506/2460-5287, 11am-midnight daily), three blocks north of the plaza. The upstairs restaurant has a terrace, with an old cast-iron stove and lanterns. The menu is heavy on surf and turf ($4-10).

Information and Services

The **Costa Rica Tourist Board** (Calle del Hogar de Ancianos, tel. 506/2461-9102, ict-sancarlos@ict.go.cr) operates a tourist bureau next to the Universidad Católica, on the northeast side of town. **CATUZON,** the Cámara de Turismo de la Zona Norte (Northern Zone Chamber of Tourism, tel.

506/2479-7512, 8am-5pm Mon.-Fri.) has an ill-stocked bureau two blocks south of the main square.

The **hospital** (tel. 506/2460-1080) is on Calle Central, about two kilometers (1.2 miles) north of the plaza. The **Red Cross** (tel. 506/2410-0599) is at Avenida 3, Calle 4. There are banks in the center of town.

Getting There

Buses (tel. 506/2255-4318 or 506/2460-5064) depart San José ($2.30) from Calle 12, Avenidas 7/9, every 45 minutes 5am-7:30pm daily; the trip takes three hours via Zarcero.

In Ciudad Quesada, the bus terminal is one block northwest of the plaza. Buses (tel. 506/2460-5032) run to La Fortuna at 6am, 10:30am, 1pm, 3:30pm, and 5pm daily; Los Chiles every two hours 5am-5pm daily; and Puerto Viejo at 6am, 10am, and 3pm daily.

You can rent cars from **Alamo Rent-a-Car** (Ave. 5, Calle Central, tel. 506/2460-0650).

CHACHAGUA

The village of Chachagua, about 20 kilometers (12 miles) west of Ciudad Quesada and 10 kilometers (6 miles) southeast of La Fortuna, is evolving as a center for ecotourism. About one kilometer (0.6 miles) east of the village, a dirt road leads to the **Chachagua Rainforest** (tel. 506/2468-1011, www.chachaguarainforesthotel.com), a 130-hectare (320-acre) private forest reserve, cattle ranch, and fruit farm nestled at the foot of the Tilarán mountain range. It has a lodge, along with a small butterfly garden and an orchid garden, and the forest is a great place for bird-watching and hiking.

Nearby, **Finca Luna Nueva Lodge** (tel. 506/2468-4006, www.fincalunanuevalodge. com) is an organic biodynamic herb farm that welcomes visitors for hikes and various tours ($20-60), plus classes ranging from the culinary arts to sustainable living. Wheelchair-accessible trails lead through a rainforest reserve, with a 15-meter-tall (50-foot-tall) observation tower. It's unsigned; take the dirt track on the south side of the highway 100 meters (330 feet) east of Restaurante Los

Piruchos del Volcán, at San Isidro de Peñas Blancas. You can overnight here.

You must visit Coco Loco Art Gallery (tel. 506/2468-0990, www.artedk.com, 8am-5pm Mon.-Sat.), five kilometers (3 miles) east of Chachagua. This exquisite German-run roadside bistro has galleries displaying the very finest Costa Rican crafts, including hammocks, exquisite marble carvings, and ceramics, plus owner Ruth Deiseroth-Kweton's own exotic, indigenous-infused art and masks.

Accommodations and Food

For chic, contemporary aesthetics in the midst of nature, check into Chachagua Rainforest Lodge (tel. 506/2468-1010, www.chachaguarainforesthotel.com, $160-240 s/d), three kilometers (2 miles) south of Chachagua. It has 22 spacious wooden cabins, each with two double beds, ceiling fans, Wi-Fi, gorgeous baths, and a deck with a picnic table and benches for enjoying the natural surroundings. The atmospheric natural-log restaurant looks out on a corral where *sabaneros* (cowboys) offer rodeo shows. There's a swimming pool, horseback riding, and nature and bird-watching hikes.

★ Finca Luna Nueva Lodge (south of Chachagua, tel. 506/2468-4006, www.fincalunanuevalodge.com, low season from $90 s, $102 d, high season from $102 s, $114 d) has a delightful eco-lodge with seven spacious air-conditioned rooms in two raised wooden structures with wraparound balconies; there are also two styles of bungalows, including family-size units. It has Wi-Fi, a spa and a solar-heated tub, and an ozonated swimming pool. The restaurant serves organic meals and will especially appeal to eco-conscious travelers.

La Fortuna to Tabacón and Arenal Volcano

The town of La Fortuna is the main gateway to Volcán Arenal, which looms to the southwest of town. Two decades ago La Fortuna was a dusty little agricultural town with potholed dirt streets. Today, it thrives on tourist traffic. In town there's not much to see except the church on the west side of the landscaped plaza, anchored by a sculpture of a volcano, but outside town the range of activities is the most concentrated in the nation, with enough to occupy visitors for a week.

West from La Fortuna, the main road begins a gradual, winding ascent to Laguna de Arenal around the northern flank of Volcán Arenal (1,670 meters/5,479 feet), some 15 kilometers (9.5 miles) from town. It's a stupendously scenic drive as you curve around Costa Rica's most active volcano. However, the volcano is often covered in clouds and getting to see an eruption is a matter of luck. The dawn hours are best, before the clouds roll in. You stand a reasonable chance in dry season, and less than favorable odds in rainy season.

MINAE's Comisión Nacional de Emergencias has set up four "safety zones" around the volcano and ostensibly regulates commercial development. It's highly arbitrary, however, and any cataclysmic eruption would devastate the entire area.

★ FINCA EDUCATIVA DON JUAN

Ebullient farmer, conservationist, educator, and former math teacher 'Don' Juan Bautista is the star of his own show at the Finca Educativa Don Juan (Don Juan Educational Farm, tel. 506/2479-8394, www.fincaeducativadonjuan.webs.com, $25 pp, by appointment), two kilometers (1.4 miles) southeast of La Fortuna at Jaúuri de Fortuna (turn south at the synthetic soccer fields, then right after 200 meters). Juan has dedicated himself to turning his one-hectare (2.5-acre) farm into

La Fortuna

To Arenal

ANCHO PIZZERIA Y RESTAURANTE

CHOZA DEL LAUREL

LUIGI'S HOTEL CASINO & RESTAURANT

LAVANDERIA LA FORTUNA

PURE TREK CANYONING/ WAVE EXPEDITIONS

Rio

GRINGO PETE'S TOO

CENTRO COMMERCIAL ADIFORT

DESAFIO

ALAMO RENT-A-CAR

LAVA LOUNGE

NATURE AIR

ARENAL CANOPY TOUR

BANK

HOTEL PARAISO TROPICAL

ARTESAN'S MARKET

CHURCH

POST OFFICE

MEGASUPER/ JACAMAR TOURS

ARENAL EVERGREEN TOURIST INFO CENTER

INTERBUS

LAVA ROCK CAFÉ/ CIUDAD QUESADA

SUPERMARKET/ BANK

RESTAURANT LA PARADA

TELEPHONES

SUPERMARKET

BUS STOP (SAN JOSE, CIUDAD QUESADA)

TAXIS

Plaza

CHOCOLATE FUSION

INTERNET

LA CASCADA

BULLRING

Burío

HOTEL LAS COLINAS

TAXIS

ADOBE RENT-A-CAR

PHARMACY

RESTAURANTE EL JARDIN

EDIFICIO VITAL/BANK

EXPEDICIONES FORTUNA

BANK

MUSMANNI

AVENTURAS

CAFÉ DON RUFINO'S

BURRUJAS LAVANDERIA

HOTEL/RESTAURANTE LA FORTUNA

HELADERÍA AND CAFETERÍA BOCATICOS

OIJ

ARENAL

BANK

PHARMACY

LA POSADA INN

GRINGO PETE'S

PANDERIA DURAN

CIRO INTERNET

BANK

CENTRO MEDICO SANAR

MEDICAL CLINIC

POLICE

SCHOOL

To El Tanque

DENTAL CLINIC

BANK

MEDICAL CLINIC

To La Cascada, Chachagua, Arenal Country Inn, and Arenal Mundo Aventuras

SCALE NOT AVAILABLE

© AVALON TRAVEL

an educational center and model for sustainable agriculture.

More than 50 crops are produced organically, and tilapia, pigs, chickens, and cattle raised and used to produce methane and fertilizer. Juan has imbued his garden with mathematical symbols. A guided interactive tour with Don Juan or one of his trained staff is an entertaining and enlightening experience as you learn the principles of organic farming, press your own fresh sugar cane juice, and sample *sobado* candy and *guaro* liquor.

The tour ends with a delicious *típica* lunch prepared over a wood-burning stove and served family style in a kitchen-restaurant overlooking the river.

You can volunteer to work here, and even stay at one of seven simple cabins on-site.

WILDLIFE PARKS

Preserve **Ecocentro Danaus Butterfly Farm and Tropical Garden** (tel. 506/2479-7019, www.ecocentrodanaus.com, 8am-4pm daily, $7, includes tour), three kilometers (2 miles) east of town, has trails through a netted butterfly garden. A separate garden features red-eyed tree frogs and poison dart frogs in re-creations of their natural environments; there are also eyelash vipers in cages.

A small lake has caimans, turtles, and waterfowl. The 6pm night walk (by reservation) is recommended.

Arenal Natura (tel. 506/2479-1616, www.arenalnatura.com, 8am-7:30pm daily, adults $35, children $17.50), six kilometers (4 miles) west of La Fortuna, offers superbly executed exhibits on frogs, snakes, butterflies, and crocodiles. The ranarium displays more than 30 frog species plus an equal number of snake species (from eyelash vipers to the dreaded fer-de-lance) in large glass cages with excellent English-language signage. Crocodiles can be viewed sloshing about in a lagoon. Night tours are offered by reservation, and well-versed guides lead tours.

The landscaped riverside **Club Rio Outdoor Center** at **The Springs Resort and Spa** (tel. 506/2401-3313, www.thespringscostarica.com, 8am-11pm daily) has a climbing and rappelling wall, tubing ($25), a ropes course, a rapids course for inflatable kayaks ($35), and horseback riding ($35). There's also a fantastic big-cat exhibit, with ocelots, margays, pumas, and jaguarundis in large landscaped cages. Some of the residents, such as Pito the ocelot, enjoy being petted; the jaguarundis spend half their time hissing at anyone who gets too close to the cage. Also here are

Arenal Volcano seen from La Fortuna

Jaguar Island, an open puma exhibit, a walk-through sloth exhibit, Monkey Island, and a snake center. It has a riverfront restaurant and bar. An all-inclusive day-pass costs $99 adults, $75 under age 12.

THEME PARKS

Ecological tropical park **Arenal Mundo Aventura** (tel. 506/2479-9762, www.arenalmundoaventura.com, 8am-5pm daily), two kilometers (1.2 miles) south of La Fortuna on the Chachagua road, is a 552-hectare (1,364-acre) rainforest reserve that offers waterfall rappelling (adults $67, children $55), zip-line tours (adults $67, children $55), horseback rides (adults $50, children $42), and nature trails with guided hikes ($35), including a nocturnal walk and guided birding (adults $48, children $39). Indigenous Malekú people demonstrate their music and dance in a traditional village.

Reserva Ecológica Catarata La Fortuna (La Fortuna Waterfall Ecological Reserve, tel. 506/2479-8338, www.arenaladifort.com, 8am-5pm daily, closed during heavy rains, $10 with guide), about four kilometers (2.5 miles) south of town, is in the care of a local community development group—the Asociación de Desarrollo Integral de La

Fortuna. The turnoff for the falls is two kilometers (1.2 miles) southeast of town, where a paved road leads uphill 2.5 kilometers (1.5 miles) to the entrance. You can view the falls in the distance from a mirador (lookout), where a slippery and precipitous trail (20 minutes' walk) leads down a steep ravine to the base of the cascade; there are steps and handrails for the steepest sections. Swimming is not advised.

Six kilometers (4 miles) west of La Fortuna, **Los Lagos Hotel Spa and Resort** (tel. 506/2479-1000, www.hotelloslagos.com, $10) has a quasi-theme park with 400 hectares (990 acres) of primary forest with trails and horseback riding, plus a ranarium (frog exhibit), crocodiles, a butterfly garden, and lush gardens with waterslides spiraling down to hot- and cold-water swimming pools. It also hosts the Canopy Tour Los Cañones.

★ HOT SPRING SPAS

Several entities make the most of the hot springs that pour from the base of the volcano. Most famous and largest of the *balnearios* (bathing resorts) is **Balneario Tabacón** (Tabacón Hot Springs, tel. 506/2519-1999, U.S. tel. 877-277-8291, www.tabacon.com, 10am-10pm daily, full-day pass with lunch or dinner

pressing sugarcane in a traditional press at Finca Educativa Don Juan

adults $85, children $30), 13 kilometers (8 miles) west of La Fortuna. It taps the steaming waters of the Río Tabacón tumbling from the lava fields to cascade alongside the road. This Spanish colonial-style *balneario* features five natural mineral pools fed by natural hot springs set in exotic, beautifully landscaped gardens, where steam rises moodily amid thick foliage. You can sit beneath waterfalls—like taking a hot shower—and lean back inside, where it feels like a sauna. The complex also has a restaurant and three bars, including a swim-up bar in the main pool. Towels, lockers, and showers are available. You'll fall in love with Tabacón by night too, when a dip becomes a romantic indulgence. I recommend the Temazcal treatment, based on an ancient indigenous steam room, at the deluxe full-service **Grand Spa** (tel. 506/2479-2028), perhaps the country's most sumptuous spa. It offers complete services in a gorgeous facility that includes open-air treatment rooms in the lush gardens. Note that Tabacón is in a high-risk zone. The former community of Tabacón was destroyed in 1968 by an eruption that killed 78 people, and in June 1975 an eruptive lava flow passed over the site of today's springs. Visitors assume their own risk.

Baldi Termae Spa (tel. 506/2479-2190, www.baldihotsprings.cr, 10am-10pm daily, day pass $31, with lunch and dinner $51), five kilometers (3 miles) west of La Fortuna, features 25 hot mineral pools, ranging 20°C to 35°C (69-95°F), lined with natural stone and landscaped with cascades and foliage. However, this Disneyesque success story can get packed—the huge spiral waterslide is a major draw, although several visitors report that it is too fast and risky. One pool has its own restaurant and deluxe hotel, two have bars, and there's a small snack bar and lockers.

I much prefer the more tranquil and tasteful **Titokú Hot Springs** (tel. 506/2479-1700, www.hotelarenalkioro.com, adults $43, children $15), immediately west of Baldi Termae. Its eight stone-lined pools vary in temperature. It has a full-service bar and buffet restaurant.

★ Arenal Waterfall Gardens

The fantastic **Arenal Waterfall Gardens,** at **The Springs Resort and Spa** (tel. 506/2401-3313, www.thespringscostarica.com, 8am-11pm daily, 24-hour pass $40, 2-day pass $50), five kilometers (3 miles) west of town, combines 19 hot spring river pools and cascades (15 more are in the works) fed by natural hot spring mineral water pumped up from 120

soaking in thermal pools at Balneario Tabacón

meters (400 feet) below ground. It uses state-of-the-art filtration to maintain water purity.

ENTERTAINMENT

The huge **Volcán Look Disco** (tel. 506/2479-9691, 8pm-3am Wed.-Sat., men $5, women free), four kilometers (2.5 miles) west of town, has a restaurant, pool tables, and Ping-Pong. Things don't stir until after 11pm.

The **Lava Lounge Bar & Grill** (tel. 506/2479-7365, www.lavaloungecostarica.com, 11am-midnight daily) is an atmospheric place to enjoy a cocktail, and also serves food. **The Springs Resort** (tel. 506/2401-3313, www.thespringscostarica.com), five kilometers (3 miles) west of town, has a tremendous game room, plus three fantastic hot spring-pool bars, accessible to nonguests with a pass (2-day pass $50).

SPORTS AND RECREATION

More than a dozen tour agencies in town offer a similar menu that includes fishing at Laguna de Arenal; trips to Volcán Arenal and Tabacón (check that the entrance fee is included in the tour price), Catarata La Fortuna, Caño Negro, and Cavernas de Venado; mountain biking; horseback trips; a safari float on the Río Peñas Blancas; and white-water rafting trips. You may be approached on the street by so-called guides, but the local chamber of commerce warns visitors "not to take tours or information off the street."

The best all-around company is **Desafío Adventure Company** (tel. 506/2479-0020, www.desafiocostarica.com), a one-stop shop for all kinds of adventures. It is particularly recommended for white-water rafting and horseback rides, as is **Don Tobias Cabalgata** (tel. 506/2479-1912, www.cabalgatadontobias.com) at Hotel Arenal Springs Resort. **Pure Trek Canyoning** (tel. 506/2479-1313, www.puretrekcostarica.com) specializes in waterfall rappelling.

Serendipity Adventures (tel. 506/2558-1000, U.S. tel. 888-226-5050, www.serendipityadventures.com, $345 pp) offers hot-air-balloon rides at dawn. Feeling flush? For a bird's-eye view of the area, take to the sky. You can rent ATVs and take ATV tours with **Powerwheels Adventures** (tel. 506/2479-1348, www.fourtraxadventure.com). **Bike Arenal** (tel. 506/2479-7150, www.bikearenal.com) offers bicycle tours.

Zip-Line Canopy Tours

For canopy tours, you're spoiled for choice.

ocelot at Arenal Waterfall Gardens

The Arenal Canopy Tour (tel. 506/2479-9769, www.canopy.co.cr, $45) offers a package that begins with a 40-minute horseback ride; you'll then whiz among 13 tree platforms using rappelling equipment. It takes two hours to traverse the circuit in a harness. Trips are offered four times daily. Ecoglide Tarzan Swing (tel. 506/2479-7120, www.arenalecoglide.com, adults $55, students and children $35), which has a 15-cable, 18-platform zip line, plus a Tarzan swing, offers trips four times daily.

Arenal Paraíso Canopy Tour (tel. 506/2460-5333, www.arenalparaiso.com, $45), at the Arenal Paraíso Hotel, has two-hour tours four times daily. Six kilometers (4 miles) west of La Fortuna, the Los Lagos Hotel (tel. 506/2479-1000, www.hotelloslagos.com) hosts the Canopy Tour Los Cañones ($25).

ACCOMMODATIONS

Every year several new hotels open. There are dozens to choose from; if they are omitted here, it does not necessarily indicate that they are not to be considered. Additional lodgings line the road between La Fortuna and El Tanque. They offer no advantages in location, however, being farther away from the volcano.

In La Fortuna

Penny-pinchers should head to Gringo Pete's (La Fortuna, tel. 506/2479-8521, www.gringopetes.com, dorms from $5 pp, private rooms from $6 pp), a rambling home-turned-hostel in lively color schemes with a choice of open-air and enclosed dorms, one with an en suite shower. Three private rooms share baths. There's a lounge with Wi-Fi, a communal kitchen, lockers, hammocks, and a barbecue grill outside. Tours are offered. It's a solid bargain. Gringo Pete also runs Gringo Pete Too, with six dorm rooms and 15 rooms with private baths.

The almost luxurious yin to Gringo Pete's yang is Arenal Backpackers' Resort (tel. 506/2479-7000, www.arenalbackpackers.com, dorm from $12 pp, camping $13, private rooms from $18 pp), with free Wi-Fi, a lovely swimming pool with a bar, and hammocks on spacious lawns. Orthopedic mattresses, silent air-conditioning, and flat-screen TVs are among the treats at this first-class budget option, three blocks west of the church.

Also setting a high standard for hostels, ★ Arenal Hostel Resort (tel. 506/2479-9222, http://arenalhostelresort.net, dorm $16 pp, private rooms $40 s, $50 d) is perhaps the nicest. Spotless, with eye-pleasing decor, it

main street in La Fortuna with Arenal Volcano in the distance

has a pool with a swim-up bar, a communal kitchen open 24-7, Wi-Fi throughout, fun activities, and even an ATM machine. It's on the main drag, one block west of the park.

In addition to the hostels above, the **Hotel Paraíso Tropical** (tel. 506/2479-9222, low season $40 s, $55 d, high season $45 s, $60 d), on the south side of the church, is one among several dozen almost identical *cabinas* in town it has 13 spacious, modestly furnished rooms with all the required amenities. Upstairs rooms are larger and have balconies with views. There's secure parking, a restaurant, a tour office, and Internet access.

Although rooms are nothing to write home about, its fine restaurant and a perfect center-of-town location are reasons enough to stay at **Luigi's Hotel & Casino** (tel. 506/2479-9636, www.luigishotel.com, low season $48 s/d, high season $60 s/d, including breakfast and tax), a two-story wooden lodge on La Fortuna's main drag. There's a pool, a whirlpool tub, Internet access, a gym, a casino, and a bar.

Outside La Fortuna

$25-50

Clean and comfortable, the well-run, no-frills **Hotel Arenal Rossi** (tel. 506/2479-9023, www.hotelarenalrossi.com, low season $36 s, $42 d, high season $40 s, $47 d, including tax and breakfast), about two kilometers (1.2 miles) west of La Fortuna, offers 25 simple but pretty *cabinas* with Wi-Fi. Rooms vary in size; one has a full kitchen. It has a steak house restaurant, plus a kids pool and swings.

$50-100

About a dozen cookie-cutter hotels in this category line the road to Tabacón. I'm partial to **Miradas Arenal** (tel. 506/2479-1944, www.miradasarenal.com, $96-125 s/d), about nine kilometers (5.5 miles) west of La Fortuna, not least for its volcano views. It has seven attractive wooden cabins amid broad lawns, and each has French doors that open to verandas.

With an enviable setting at a higher elevation than any other hotel in the region, the **Arenal Observatory Lodge & Spa** (tel. 506/2479-1070, reservations tel. 506/2290-7011, www.arenalobservatorylodge.com, $94-151 s/d) sits on the slopes of Cerro Chato—a smaller and extinct volcano immediately east of Volcán Arenal. Stay here for stupendous views over the lake and the volcano. It was built in 1987 as an observatory for the Smithsonian Institute and the University of Costa Rica. Today it has 40 rooms of three types in four widely dispersed buildings. The modestly furnished but comfortable standard rooms have twin beds and sliding glass doors that open to volcano-view balconies. Four observatory rooms have volcano views through vast picture windows, as do nine spacious superior rooms in the Smithsonian block, reached via a suspension bridge. Five luxury junior suites are more graciously furnished and have the best views. Five rooms are wheelchair-accessible. A converted farmhouse, **La Casona** ($63 s/d), 500 meters (0.3 miles) away, accommodates 14 more guests in four rooms with shared baths (only three rooms have volcano views). The **White Hawk Villa** accommodates 10 people (from $510). The lodge offers horseback rides, hikes, and free canoeing on Lake Chato. There's a splendid walk-in infinity swimming pool, plus a whirlpool tub, a kids pool, and a bar.

$100-150

For seclusion and great volcano views, you can't beat **Lomas del Volcán** (tel. 506/2479-9000, www.lomasdelvolcan.com, low season $120 s, $130 d, high season $130 s, $135 d), amid dairy pastures about one kilometer (0.6 miles) off the main road, four kilometers (2.5 miles) west of town. It has 13 spacious wooden stilt cabins, some with king beds, and all with glass-enclosed porches. Nature trails lead into the forest. Horses can be rented, and there's Wi-Fi in the reception area.

With its stone-faced reception area, **Volcano Lodge** (tel. 506/2479-1717, www.volcanolodge.com, low season $115 s/d, high season $150 s/d), about six kilometers (4 miles) west of town, offers 20 beautifully appointed two-bedroom cottages with large picture windows as well as porches with rockers for enjoying the volcano views beyond the gardens, which have a lovely swimming pool with swim-up bar. Choose a king bed or two queens. Facilities include a pool and a whirlpool tub, and intermittent Wi-Fi. The restaurant is one of the finest around.

Another of my near-identical faves is the hillside **Montaña de Fuego Resort & Spa** (tel. 506/2479-1220, www.montanadefuego.com, $150 s/d), with 66 handsome hardwood air-conditioned *cabinas* and bungalow suites with splendid volcano views through glass-enclosed verandas (many rooms face away from the volcano). The hotel has a glass-enclosed restaurant, a swimming pool, a spa, and a zipline canopy.

OVER $150

By far the most dramatic hotel is ★ **The Springs Resort & Spa** (tel. 506/2401-3313, www.thespringscostarica.com, low season from $445 s/d, high season from $490 s/d), five kilometers (3 miles) west of La Fortuna. This deluxe all-suite property (an episode of the TV series *The Bachelor* was filmed here) is particularly fun for families for its hot springs, wildlife draws, and riverside activities. The six-story main building is built on a hillside, with tiered hot springs landscaped into grottos, waterfalls, and pools. The suites, in separate blocks, all have wall-of-glass volcano views from raised king beds. Hallmarks that delight include huge flat-screen TVs, iPod docks, DVD players, luxurious furnishings, and sumptuous marble-clad baths with walk-in showers and separate his-and-hers whirlpool tubs. Plus you get direct access to its Arenal Waterfall Gardens for free.

The upscale, nonsmoking **Tabacón Lodge** (tel. 506/2479-2000, www.tabacon.com, from $255 s/d year-round), 200 meters (660 feet) uphill of Balneario Tabacón, is set amid lush well-maintained gardens. The property has 73 air-conditioned rooms, all with beautiful Georgian-inspired mahogany furnishings, king beds, 40-inch flat-screen TVs, marble-clad baths, and a patio affording a volcano

view. Nine rooms are junior suites with private garden whirlpool tubs. There's a small gym, a gourmet restaurant, a swim-up bar in a hot spring pool, and the luxurious Grand Spa at the *balneario*. Rates include breakfast and unlimited access to the *balneario*.

Taking the prize for audacious locale is the all-suite **Arenal Kioro** (tel. 506/2479-1700, www.hotelarenalkioro.com, low season from $209 s, $239 d, high season from $335 s, $385 d), at the very base of the volcano. Its 53 spacious and graciously appointed air-conditioned suites have walls of glass, lush contemporary furnishings, marble-clad baths, and en-suite whirlpool tub with volcano views. There's a full-service spa, a gym, and two hot spring swimming pools, while the superb Restaurante Heliconias enjoys a grandstand view. If the volcano erupts, you might find yourself too close for comfort.

Earning laurels from major travel magazines, ★ **Arenal Nayara Hotel & Gardens** (tel. 506/2479-1600, www.arenalnayara.com, $280-590 s/d year-round), five miles west of La Fortuna, is perhaps the most romantic and stylish hotel for miles. It's inspired by Balinese architecture and makes tremendous use of Indonesian hardwood furnishings. The huge, gracious guest rooms have lively color schemes (lime green, tangerine) and a traditional feel melding with flat-screen TVs and other contemporary touches. Most rooms have king beds, many canopied, and all come with a panoply of modern amenities, plus raised bamboo ceilings and large glass French doors opening to balconies with whirlpool tubs. The stylish baths have indoor and outdoor showers. The restaurant is one of the best around. Arenal Nayara is truly lovely.

FOOD
In La Fortuna

The thatched-roof **Rancho La Cascada Restaurant** (tel. 506/2479-9145, 6am-11pm daily), on the north side of the plaza, serves filling breakfasts, plus *típico* and eclectic dishes, such as burgers and pastas ($2-6).

For traditional local fare, head to **Choza**

de Laurel (tel. 506/2479-7063, www.lachozadelaurel.com, 6:30am-10pm daily), a rustic Tican country inn with cloves of garlic hanging from the roof and an excellent *plato especial*—a mixed plate of Costa Rican dishes. Grilled chicken ($2-6) and *casados* (set lunches, $4) are other good bets, served by waitresses in traditional costume.

For elegance, I opt for Restaurante Luigi (tel. 506/2479-9698, 6am-11pm daily), two blocks west of the plaza. This airy upscale option lists a large pasta and pizza menu, plus the likes of bruschetta ($5), cream of mushroom soup ($4), beef stroganoff ($10), and sea bass with shrimp ($15). It specializes in flambé and has a large cocktail list.

Some of the best eats in town are at ★ Don Rufino (tel. 506/2479-9997, www.donrufino.com, 7am-11pm daily), one block east of the plaza. Airy and elegant, it offers a wide menu that ranges from veggies on the grill ($6) to filet mignon ($15) or porterhouse with gorgonzola sauce ($18); the house special is *pollo al estilo de la abuela* (grandma's chicken). It serves great *bocas* at the bar and is the town's unofficial epicenter of social life.

The restaurant at Arenal Observatory Lodge (tel. 506/2479-1070, www.arenalobservatorylodge.com) is open to nonguests and serves breakfast (7am-8:30am daily), lunch (11:30am-4:30pm daily), and dinner (6pm-8:30pm daily). The food is tasty and filling, but you're here for the magnificent vantage point.

For ice cream, head to Heladería Bocatico (tel. 506/2479-9576), on the plaza's east side. This open-air restaurant has a hip, modern motif with a bamboo ceiling and stainless-steel chairs on a wooden deck.

Outside La Fortuna

The upscale Los Tucanes Restaurant (Tabacón Lodge, uphill from Balneario Tabacón, tel. 506/2479-2000, www.tabacon.com, 6:30am-10:30am and 5pm-10pm daily) offers magnificent volcano views. I like its chic contemporary styling and the views over a lovely swimming pool with a cascade. The menu spans the globe with such treats as sautéed escargots ($26) and roasted salmon with truffle-oil mashed potatoes ($28).

An upscale standout south of town, the elegant ★ Restaurante Heliconias (tel. 506/2479-1700, www.hotelarenalkioro.com, 6:30am-10pm daily), in the Arenal Kioro hotel, is right below the lava flows. Its position is spectacular, with a wall of glass that opens so you can even hear the lava while you dine. The cuisine also rates well. Begin, perhaps, with the octopus cocktail ($12) or *pejibaye* cream ($6) followed by sea bass in caper sauce ($16), and perhaps the seafood salad made at your table with 12 ingredients.

★ Altamira (tel. 506/2479-1600, www.arenalnayara.com, 6:30am-10am, 11am-2pm, and 5:30pm-10pm daily), at the Arenal Nayara Hotel, five miles west of La Fortuna, is no less stylish, blending a Balinese theme into a contemporary style. Gazpacho ($6), ceviche, mushroom gratin, beef jalapeño tenderloin ($16), and seafood Pernod ($18) exemplify the menu. Dine beneath a huge *palenque* roof hung with Chinese lanterns. The hotel also serves Latin fusion dishes plus sushi in its Sushi Amor restaurant, done up incongruously with traditional Costa Rican decor.

INFORMATION AND SERVICES

The Clínica La Fortuna (tel. 506/2479-9142, 7am-5pm Mon.-Fri., 7am-noon Sat.) is two blocks northeast of the gas station. The private Clínica Médico Sanar (tel. 506/2479-9420), two blocks east of the plaza, has an ambulance service. The Arenal Dental Clinic (tel. 506/2579-9696) is one block southeast of the school, with Consultorio Médico (tel. 506/2479-8911) opposite.

The police station (tel. 506/2479-9689) is on the north side of the school; for the tourist police, call tel. 506/2479-7257. The OIJ (criminal investigation, tel. 506/2579-7225) office is on the main drag, one block east of the plaza.

There are three banks in town, and more Internet cafés than you can shake a stick at, including **Ciro Internet** (tel. 506/2479-7769) on the main drag opposite the school. Head to **Lavandería La Fortuna** (tel. 506/2479-9547, 8am-9pm Mon.-Sat.), one block west of the plaza, or **Burruja Lavandería** (opposite Hotel Fortuna, tel. 506/2479-7115, 7am-10pm daily) for laundry.

GETTING THERE AND AROUND

Autotransportes San Carlos (tel. 506/2255-0567) buses depart San José ($3) from Calle 12, Avenidas 7/9, at 6:15am, 8:40am, and 11:30am daily. Return buses depart La Fortuna from the south side of the plaza at 12:45pm and 2:45pm daily. Buses (tel. 506/2460-3480) depart Ciudad Quesada for La Fortuna ($1.05) 13 times daily at irregular hours. **Interbus** (tel. 506/4100-0888, www.interbusonline.com) and **Grayline Costa Rica** (tel. 506/2220-2126, www.graylinecostarica.com) operate shuttles from San José ($35) and popular tourist destinations in Nicoya and Guanacaste.

Alamo (tel. 506/2479-9090, www.alamocostarica.com) has a car rental office on the main drag in La Fortuna. **Bike Rental Arenal** (tel. 506/2479-7150, www.bikearenal.com), seven kilometers (4.5 miles) south of town, rents mountain bikes ($22 daily, $132 weekly). **Segway Costa Rica** (tel. 506/2479-8736, www.segwaycostarica.com, over age 7, $39) offers tours of the town by Segway glider at 9am, 1pm, and 4pm daily.

★ ARENAL VOLCANO NATIONAL PARK

The 12,016-hectare (29,692-acre) **Parque Nacional Volcán Arenal** (tel. 506/8775-2943 or 506/2461-8499, www.sinac.go.cr, 8am-4pm daily, last entrance at 3pm except with local guide, $10) lies within the 204,000-hectare (500,000-acre) Arenal Conservation Area, a polyglot assemblage protecting 16 reserves in the region between the Guanacaste and Tilarán mountain ranges, and including Laguna de Arenal. The park has two volcanoes: extinct Chato (1,140 meters/3,740 feet),

Arenal Volcano

whose collapsed crater contains an emerald lagoon, and active Arenal (1,633 meters/5,358 feet), a picture-perfect cone.

Hiking too close to the volcano is not advisable. Heed the warning signs—the volcano is totally unpredictable, and there is a strong possibility of losing your life if you venture into restricted zones.

Arenal slumbered peacefully throughout the colonial era. On July 29, 1968, it was awakened from its long sleep with a fateful earthquake. The massive explosion that resulted wiped out the villages of Tabacón and Pueblo Nuevo. The blast was felt as far away as Boulder, Colorado. Thereafter its lava flows and eruptions were relatively constant, and on virtually any day you could see smoking cinder blocks tumbling down the steep slope from the horseshoe-shaped crater—or at night, watch a fiery cascade of lava spewing from the 140-meter-deep (460-foot-deep) crater. Some days the volcano blew several times in an hour, spewing house-size rocks, sulfur dioxide, chloride gases, and red-hot lava. The

Arenal Volcano National Park

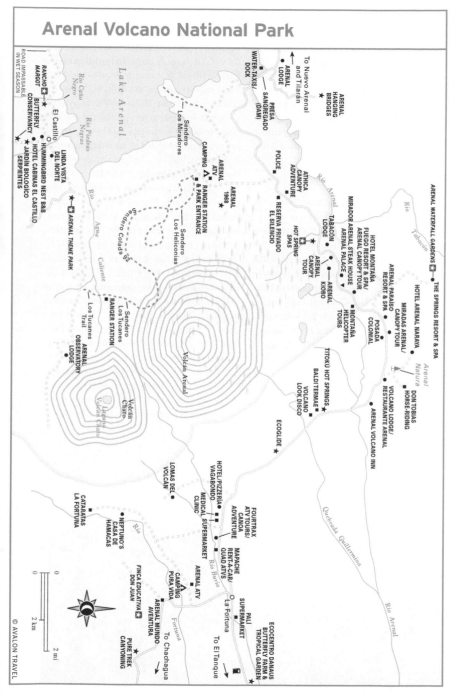

© AVALON TRAVEL

volcano's active vent often shifts location; for the past decade it has been on the northern side, but in 2008 a collapse at the crater rim shifted the predominant lava flows to the southern side. Explosions and eruptions, however, occur on all sides.

The volcano entered a particularly active phase in 2005, with an average of five to eight "big boom" explosions daily. In September 2010 it suddenly went quiet, but since 2013 has been intermittently active.

Park Trails

The one-kilometer (0.6-mile) **Las Heliconias Trail** leads from the ranger station past an area where vegetation is recolonizing the 1968 lava flow. The trail intersects the **Look-Out Point Trail,** which leads 1.3 kilometers (0.8 miles) from the ranger station to a mirador—a viewing area—from which you can watch active lava flowing. **Las Coladas Trail** begins at the intersection and leads 2.8 kilometers (1.7 miles) to a lava flow from 1993. The **Los Miradores Trail** begins at park headquarters and leads 1.2 kilometers (0.75 miles) to Laguna de Arenal.

Reserva Privada El Silencio (tel. 506/2479-9900, 7am-9pm daily, $5), 500 meters (0.3 miles) east of the turnoff for the national park, has a three-kilometer (2-mile) trail. You can even drive up to a lookout beneath the flow. The closest hiking to the lava flows (and the only one offering hikes on the big lava flows), is at nearby **Arenal 1968** (tel. 506/2462-1212, 8am-7pm daily, $15), near the entrance to Parque Nacional Volcán Arenal. Oropendolas and parrots inhabit the *guayaba* trees festooned with epiphytes in the parking lot, near a mirador that offers sweeping vistas. A steep trail leads up the four-decade-old lava flow. It's a fabulous hike! The full loop trail takes you past a grotto that is a shrine to those who died in 1968. The 4.5-kilometer (3-mile) Forest Hike leads through a wooded area ringing a small lake created by the 1968 eruption. It also has mountain bike and horse trails.

You can also hike at the **Arenal Observatory Lodge** (tel. 506/2479-1070, www.arenalobservatorylodge.com). A guided hike is offered at 8:30am daily (complimentary to guests). The four-kilometer (2.5-mile) Lava Trail (a tough climb back to the lodge—don't believe your guide if they say it's easy) is free and takes about three hours round-trip. The Chato Trail (4 hours) is longer and more difficult. The Arenal Observatory Lodge has a small but interesting **Museum of Volcanology.**

Outside the entrance to the lodge is the

hikers in Arenal Volcano National Park

trailhead for the private **Los Tucanes Trail** (self-guided, 8am-8pm daily, $4), which leads to the southernmost lava flows (1 hour one-way). **Arenal ATV** (tel. 506/2479-8643, www.originalarenalatv.com), opposite the park entrance gate, has ATV tours ($89) at 7:30am, 11:30am, and 2:30pm daily.

No camping is allowed in the park. However, you can camp on land adjacent to the ranger station ($2.50 pp), with basic toilets and showers.

Getting There

The turnoff to the park entrance is 2.5 kilometers (1.5 miles) west of Tabacón and 3.5 kilometers (2 miles) east of the Laguna de Arenal dam. The dirt access road leads 1.5 kilometers (0.9 miles) to the ranger station, which gives a small informational pamphlet and has restrooms. A dirt road leads north from here 1.5 kilometers (0.9 miles) to a parking lot and hiking trails.

Laguna de Arenal

Picture-perfect Laguna de Arenal might have been transplanted from England's Lake District, surrounded as it is by emerald-green mountains. The looming mass of Volcán Arenal rises over the lake to the east. About 2 to 3 million years ago, tectonic movements created a depression that filled with a small lagoon. In 1973, the Costa Rican electric utility company, ICE, built an 88-meter-long (289-foot-long), 56-meter-tall (184-foot-tall) dam with an electricity-generating station at the eastern end of the valley, creating a narrow 32-kilometer-long (20-mile-long) reservoir

covering 12,400 hectares (30,640 acres). High winds whip up whitecaps, providing thrills for wind- and kite-surfers, and powering the huge turbines that stud the mountain ridge southwest of the lake. Warning: Crocodiles have been seen in the lake in recent years. Don't ask me how they got there!

The only town is **Nuevo Arenal,** a small pueblo on the north-central shore, 32 kilometers (20 miles) northeast of Tilarán, immediately west of the Guanacaste-Alajuela provincial boundary. It was created in 1973 when the artificial lake flooded the original

Arenal Volcano from Laguna de Arenal

Laguna de Arenal

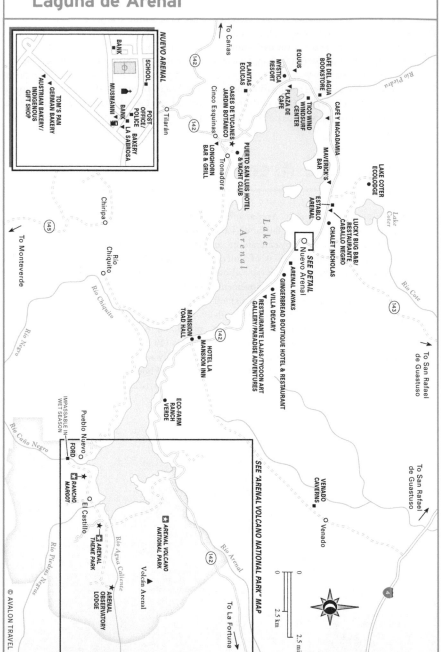

NUEVO ARENAL

BANK ■
SCHOOL ■
POST OFFICE/ POLICE ■
BANK ■ BAKERY
LA SABROSA
MUSMANNI ▼ ■
TOM'S PAN ▼
GERMAN BAKERY ▼
AUSTRIAN BAKERY/ INDIGENOUS GIFT SHOP

To Cañas

Río Piedra

CAFÉ DEL AGUA BOOKSTORE ■
CAFÉ Y MACADAMIA
EQUUS ▼
MYSTICA RESORT ▼
PLANTAS EÓLICAS ■
PLAZA DE CAFÉ ■
TICO WIND WINDSURF CENTER ■
OASES DE TUCANES ■
JARDIN BOTÁNICO
Cinco Esquinas ○
Tilarán ○

MAVERICK'S BAR ■

LAKE COTER ECOLODGE ●
Lake Coter

LUCKY BUG B&B/ RESTAURANTE CABALLO NEGRO ●
ESTABLO ARENAL ■
CHALET NICHOLAS ●

PUERTO SAN LUIS HOTEL & YACHT CLUB ⚓
Tronadora
LONGHORN BAR & GRILL ▼

Lake Arenal

Chiripa ○

To Monteverde

Río Chiquito ○

Río Chiquito

Río Negro

MANSION TOAD HALL ■
MANSION LA MANSION INN ●
HOTEL LA MANSION INN ●

SEE DETAIL
○ Nuevo Arenal
■ ARENAL KAYAKS
● GINGERBREAD BOUTIQUE HOTEL & RESTAURANT
▼ VILLA DECARY
▼ RESTAURANTE LAJAS/TYCOON ART GALLERY/PARADISE ADVENTURES

Río Cote

To San Rafael de Guastuso

ECO-FARM RANCH VERDE ●

IMPASSABLE IN WET SEASON
Pueblo Nuevo ○
FORD ■

Río Caño Negro

RANCHO MARGOT ★

○ El Castillo

Río Piedras Negras

ARENAL THEME PARK ★
ARENAL VOLCANO NATIONAL PARK ★
Volcán Arenal ▲
ARENAL OBSERVATORY LODGE ★

Río Agua Caliente

VENADO CAVERNS ■

○ Venado

To San Rafael de Guastuso

SEE "ARENAL VOLCANO NATIONAL PARK" MAP

Río Arenal

To La Fortuna

0   2.5 km
0   2.5 mi

© AVALON TRAVEL

eyelash viper, Arenal Hanging Bridges

Coter, a small lake five kilometers (3 miles) northwest of Nuevo Arenal.

On the south side, the paved road continues east only as far as Tronadora, beyond which it turns to dirt and eventually peters out. You cannot get through to La Fortuna, or El Castillo—a community with accommodations and attractions on the lake's southeast. El Castillo is reached via the dirt road that passes the entrance to Parque Nacional Volcán Arenal. El Castillo was pretty badly shaken by the September 2012 earthquake, and many properties were badly damaged.

SIGHTS

Arenal Hanging Bridges (tel. 506/2290-0469, 8am-4:30pm daily, last entrance 3:30pm, adults $24, seniors $19, students $14), within a 250-hectare (618-acre) reserve immediately east of the dam, provides a marvelous introduction to forest ecology as you follow a three-kilometer (2-mile) self-guided interpretive trail with 15 sturdy bridges, some up to 100 meters (330 feet) long, suspended across ravines and treetops. Guided tours include an early-morning bird-watching tour (adults $47, seniors $42, students $37). You get great volcano views.

The Butterfly Conservancy (tel. 506/2479-1149, www.butterflyconservatory. org, 8:30am-4:30pm daily, adults $12, under age 8 and students $8) at El Castillo is a butterfly garden and insect museum with live scorpions, rhinoceros beetles, and lizards, among other creatures. About 30 species of butterflies are raised here and flit beneath seven netted arenas, claimed to be the largest in Costa Rica, while others are released to repopulate the wild. It also has a poison dart frog exhibit, a botanical garden with medicinal plants, and trails good for viewing monkeys. Next door, Victor Hugo Quesada's **Jardín Biológico y Serpientes del Arenal** (tel. 506/8358-6773, 8am-9pm daily, low season $12, high season $15) has an excellent snake exhibit with about 35 species, including pit vipers and fer-de-lance, plus poison dart frogs, lizards, turtles, and arachnids. The **Arenal Ecozoo**

settlement, and now occupies a ridge of prime real estate with gorgeous views. This is the only place to gas up and use an ATM.

The lake is easily reached from La Fortuna, 20 kilometers (12 miles) east of the dam, or from Cañas on the Pan-American Highway via Tilarán. The paved road swings around the north and west side of the lake, linking the two towns. The section east of Nuevo Arenal is backed by thick rainforest and is one of the prettiest drives in Costa Rica, with a fistful of eclectic restaurants and bed-and-breakfasts dotting the route. Animals such as coatis are often present, begging for food (don't feed the wildlife). I've even seen a peccary crossing the road. Landslides are a frequent occurrence and often close the road east of Nuevo Arenal for days at a time; at best, expect some washed-out sections.

A dirt road that begins just east of Hotel La Mansion Inn leads over the cordillera to Cavernas de Venado. Another road leads north from just west of Nuevo Arenal to San Rafael de Guatuso; a fork leads past Lago (tel. 506/2479-1059, www.arenalecozoo.com, 8am-7pm daily, adults $15, students and children $10), a stone's throw away, has hopped on the bandwagon and offers its own butterfly garden, serpentarium, insectarium, ranarium, and insect exhibits.

★ Rancho Margot

Rancho Margot (tel. 506/8302-7318, www.ranchomargot.com), on the banks of the Río Caño Negro, at the end of the dirt road west of El Castillo, is a fascinating self-sufficient organic farm, an ecological activity center, and a kibbutz-like teaching community based on sustainable rural tourism and conservation. Pigs and cattle are raised; prosciutto, cheeses, and other products are made on-site; and visitors can participate in farm activities. It's based around an ivy-clad farmstead in traditional colonial style. Educational tours are offered; you'll get to see the pig-waste compost heater, which provides the methane that heats a swimming pool, and learn why it doesn't stink. Activities include horseback riding ($35-50), kayaking ($40), rappelling ($55), and hiking ($20) on the property's 152 hectares (376 acres) of forest bordering the Children's Eternal Rainforest Reserve. It also hosts twice-daily yoga plus Spanish-language programs,

and has a wildlife rehabilitation center housing deer and monkeys. *Comida típica* meals are served hot from the stove. The ranch operates its own bus from the plaza in La Fortuna at 7am, noon, and 5:45pm daily.

★ Arenal Theme Park

Want to fly through the air with the greatest of ease while enjoying spectacular views? **Arenal Theme Park** (tel. 506/2479-4100, www.skyadventures.travel, 7:30am-5pm daily), immediately east of El Castillo, on the north-facing slopes of the Cordillera de Tilarán, offers phenomenal volcano vistas, to be enjoyed from an aerial **Sky Tram** (adults $44, students $38, children $28) that rises 236 meters (774 feet) to takes visitors up to a mirador (lookout) The mirador is the beginning of the **Sky Trek** (adults $77, students $61, children $48, including tram) zip-line circuit, with 2.8 kilometers (1.7 miles) of zip lines stretching across canyons and between treetops. There's also a **Sky Walk** by suspension bridges, and a white-water **Sky Drift.**

ENTERTAINMENT

Who'd have thought such a wild and wacky disco would be found here, but when Saturday comes around, don't miss

spider monkey with youngster, Arenal Hanging Bridges

the **Equus Disco,** an open-air stone-lined party palace surrounded by dense foliage and giant rocks. It's located one kilometer west of Mystica Resort. Even the local howler monkeys are known to howl to the music. It has a huge video screen.

SPORTS AND RECREATION

Hacienda Toad Hall (tel. 506/2692-8063, www.toadhallarenal.com), about six kilometers (4 miles) east of Nuevo Arenal, rents horses and offers horseback riding. **Rancho Margot** (tel. 506/8302-7318, www.ranchomargot.com), on the banks of the Río Caño Negro, at the end of the dirt road west of El Castillo, also rents horses, offers horseback riding, and has kayaking.

Windsurfing and Water Sports

In the morning the lake can look like a mirror, but the calm is short-lived. More normal are nearly constant 30- to 80-km/h (20-50 mph) winds, which whip up whitecaps and turn the lake into one of the world's top windsurfing spots. Swells can top one meter (3 feet). Forty km/h (25 mph) is the *average* winter day's wind speed. November, December, and January are the best months for windsurfing; September and October are worst.

Englishman Peter Hopley runs the **Tico Wind Surf Center** (western shore, tel. 506/2692-2002, www.ticowind.com, 9am-6pm daily Dec.-Apr.). Peter uses state-of-the-art equipment, has a great lineup of gear, and offers instruction in several languages. One-hour beginner lessons cost $50; a full nine-hour course costs $480. Board rentals are from $15 per hour, $42 half-day. You need a 4WD vehicle for access.

Paradise Adventures (tel. 506/8856-3618, www.paradise-adventures-costa-rica.com) spices up the experience with wakeboarding behind speedboats—it's like snowboarding on water. Owner Jonny T brings in world champs as instructors. **Fly Zone** (tel. 506/8339-5876, www.flyzone-cr.com) has similar offerings.

Arenal Kayaks (tel. 506/2694-4366, www.arenalkayaks.com), about one kilometer (0.6 miles) east of Nuevo Arenal, rents kayaks and has guided trips using handcrafted wooden kayaks made on-site.

Fishing and Lake Tours

The lake is stocked with game fish—*guapote, machaca,* and for lighter-tackle enthusiasts, *mojarra.* Most of the hotels hereabouts offer fishing tours, as does **Captain Ron's Laguna de Arenal Fishing Tours** (tel. 506/2694-4678, www.arenalfishing.com), in Nuevo Arenal. **Puerto San Luis Lodge & Yacht Club** (tel. 506/2695-5750, www.hotelpuertosanluiscr.com) rents out 8- and 20-passenger boats for fishing and lake tours.

The *Rain Goddess* (U.S. tel. 317-408-5942, www.arenalhouseboattours.com) is a deluxe 65-foot live-aboard vessel that operates three-hour lake tours (4 hours, $100 pp) at 4pm daily, with dinner optional. You can also charter the boat and customize your own program; it sleeps eight.

SHOPPING

The **Lucky Bug Gallery** (tel. 506/2694-4515, www.luckybugcr.net, 7am-5pm daily), two kilometers (1.2 miles) west of Nuevo Arenal, sells a fabulous array of quality custom crafts, from metal insects and naked fairy lamps to masks, exquisite hammered tin pieces, and ceramics. Many of the fabulous works are by owners Monica and Willy Krauskopf's triplets: Alexandra, Katherine, and Sabrina. They will ship oversize pieces.

Likewise, the venerable **Toad Hall** (tel. 506/2692-8063, www.toadhallarenal.com, 8:30am-6pm daily), six kilometers (4 miles) east of Nuevo Arenal, sells a huge range of quality souvenirs and has a top-notch café.

Casa Delagua (tel. 506/2692-2101, goodell50@gmail.com, 8am-sunset daily), on the northwest shore, hosts an art gallery selling superb works by, not least, artist Juan Carlos Ruiz, plus books and music DVDs.

ACCOMMODATIONS

Hotels are predominantly along the north shore. There are many more to choose from, but these are my pick of the litter.

El Castillo

One of few true budget options in the area, **Essence Arenal** (tel. 506/2479-1131, www.essencearenal.com, camping $5, tent $28, rooms $28-48 s/d), set on 22 hectares (54 acres) of forested grounds one kilometer (0.6 miles) south of El Castillo, is a backpackers hostel and tent resort. The tents are safari-style, on decks; deluxe tents have private baths. A huge hearth keeps things warm in the lounge, and there's a TV room, a pool, free Internet access, and movie nights. It also has double, triple, and quad rooms, all with orthopedic mattresses. Chef Isaac Weliver prepares gourmet vegetarian dishes.

For intimacy in El Castillo, opt for former Pan Am flight attendant Ellen Neely's lovely **Hummingbird Nest B&B** (tel. 506/8835-8711, www.hummingbirdnestbb.com, 2-night minimum, $55 s, $85 d, includes tax and breakfast), set in hilltop gardens. You get fabulous volcano views through picture windows in its two guest rooms; baths are a bit small. All rooms have ceiling fans, mini fridges, and homey decor such as frilly pillows. It has a patio whirlpool tub. Hummingbird Nest is a solid bargain.

Rancho Margot (tel. 506/8302-7318, www.ranchomargot.com, 2-night minimum, bunkhouse $70 pp, all-inclusive; bungalows $149 pp, including meals) has bunks in basic yet clean and well-thought-out dorm rooms with shared baths. There are 18 lovely bungalows at the forest's edge, nicely furnished and boasting terra-cotta floors, whitewashed walls, modern baths, and spacious decks. Prices include a tour, yoga, and some activities. The Sunday buffet draws locals from far and wide—no wonder, as a professional chef attends to the kitchen.

North and West Shore

American owners Jeff and Bill make you feel right at home in **Villa Decary** (tel. 506/2694-4330 or 800-556-0505, www.villadecary.com, low season $99-149 s/d, high season $109-164, cash only), a small country inn on a former fruit and coffee finca on three hilly hectares (7 acres) between Nuevo Arenal and the botanical gardens. The contemporary two-story structure glows with light. Hardwood furniture gleams. Five large bedrooms have bright Guatemalan covers, plus a balcony with a handy rail that serves as a bench and a table. Three new *cabinas* are perched farther up the hill. The gardens and surrounding forest are great for bird-watching. The hotel is gay-friendly and has Wi-Fi. No credit cards are accepted. Rates include full breakfast.

Gourmands will appreciate the Israeli-owned **Gingerbread Boutique Hotel & Restaurant** (tel. 506/2694-0039, www.gingerbreadarenal.com, low season $95 s/d, high season $110 s/d), three kilometers (2 miles) east of Nuevo Arenal. The stone-clad gourmet restaurant is the main reason to stay here. It has five exquisitely decorated air-conditioned rooms with cable TV, phones, Wi-Fi, and ceiling fans, plus colorful art and themed wall murals; the windowless air-conditioned wine cellar had blood-red walls and a garden shower.

Lovers of New Mexico styling will feel right at home at ★ **Hacienda Toad Hall** (tel. 506/2692-8063, U.S. tel. 800-796-0471, www.toadhallarenal.com, from $75 s/d), about eight kilometers (5 miles) east of Nuevo Arenal. The magnificent creation of Jeff and Lydia Van Mill from Arizona, it's done up in gorgeous sepia tones and has a breeze-swept pool and a sundeck with views. Choose from the two-bedroom hacienda, a two-bedroom bi-level villa, a single-bedroom *cabina,* or the Jungle Suite, all tastefully furnished with rustic antiques and flat-screen TVs. The couple offer horseback tours, plus you get the superb café-restaurant next door.

I love the hillside **Mystica Resort** (tel. 506/2692-1001, www.mysticacostarica.com, rooms $90 s, $120 d, villa $165), run by an Italian couple. Set in lush grounds on the west shore, it offers six large, simply furnished rooms in pastel earth tones with king beds, thick comforters, and luxurious linens. Sit on your veranda and admire the landscaped grounds cascading to the lake below and Volcán Arenal in the distance. Gourmet dinners are served in a high-ceilinged restaurant specializing in pizzas. It has a yoga deck, a landscaped swimming pool, and a massage room. A romantic private villa has a kitchen and a fireplace. Rates include breakfast.

Friendly Great Danes welcome guests to the delightful American-run ★ **Chalet Nicholas** (tel./fax 506/2694-4041, www.chaletnicholas.com, low season $67 s/d, high season $77 s/d, cash only), a splendid three-bedroom Colorado-style guesthouse two kilometers (1.2 miles) west of Nuevo Arenal. Run by live-in owners Catherine and John Nichola, it exudes charm and all the comforts of home. Two bedrooms are downstairs. A spiral staircase winds up to a larger semiprivate loft bedroom with a cozy sitting area boasting a deck good for bird-watching. All rooms have volcano views. It has a TV lounge, a fruit orchard, an orchid house, and hiking and horseback riding into an adjacent forest reserve. The organic meals get rave reviews. Rates include

breakfast—perhaps Cathy's macadamia-nut pancakes served with fresh fruit. Smoking is not allowed, and credit cards are not accepted.

By far the most sumptuous hotel hereabouts is the hillside **Hotel La Mansion Inn** (tel. 506/2692-8018, www.lamansion-arenal.com, low season $135-595 s/d, high season $195-995 s/d), next to Toad Hall. Bougainvillea clambers over 16 *cabinas* with lake views, wrought-iron furniture, mezzanine bedrooms with king beds, and French doors that open to verandas with Sarchí rockers. Five luxury rooms take the decor to new heights. The luxe Royal Honeymoon Suite and Royal Cottage sleep up to six. An open-air bar is shaped like a ship's bow, and the restaurant is nautically themed. There's a spring-fed infinity pool, horseback riding, canoes, and rowboats. Rates include breakfast and horseback riding.

FOOD

At El Castillo, be sure to go for pizza or just a laugh from John DaVita, a former LA punk rocker who runs ★ **Pizza John's Jardín Escondido** (tel. 506/2479-1155, noon-9pm daily), tucked away off the road to Rancho Margot; keep an eye out for the sign. John loves to tell outrageous tales, but also cooks

photographing coatis near Lake Arenal

up a mean pizza and delicious homemade ice cream.

Moving along the north shore, for breakfast I head to ★ **Tom's Pan** (tel. 506/2694-4547, www.tomspan.com, 7:30am-4pm Mon.-Sat. low season, 7:30am-5:30pm daily high season), in Nuevo Arenal. This delightfully rustic German-run outdoor café is splendid for enjoying American breakfasts. It also has sandwiches, beef stew with veggies, dumplings with bacon, sauerkraut, chicken with rice, roast pork with homemade noodles, Tom's pastries, and other splendid baked goods. Competing next door, the **Austrian Bakery** (tel. 506/2694-4445, 8am-5pm daily) is more contemporary and serves fabulous bread, croissants, and cappuccinos, among other treats. It also has a tremendous crafts store.

In pizza mode, on the west shore the charming restaurant at **Mystica Resort** (tel. 506/2692-1001, noon-9pm daily) has a splendid Italian menu that includes 16 types of pizza (from $8), plus pastas, and a large Italian wine list, served in front of a cozy hearth.

Levantine dishes feature on the menu at the Tuscan-style ★ **Gingerbread** (Gingerbread Boutique Hotel, tel. 506/2694-0039, www.gingerbreadarenal.com, 5pm-9pm Tues.-Sat., $20), three kilometers (2 miles) east of Nuevo Arenal, with a daily menu that can also include filet mignon, jumbo shrimp with couscous and lentils, and tuna sashimi. Israeli owner-chef Eyal Ben-Menachem really knows how to deliver mouthwatering fare.

A more contemporary alternative, **Gallery y Restaurante Lajas** (tel. 506/2694-4780, lajasdesinet@racsa.co.cr, 8am-5pm daily), 300 meters (1,000 feet) east of Villa Decary, serves a great *gallo pinto,* sandwiches, salads, soups, seafood dishes, espressos, and cappuccinos on an open-air veranda. Carlos, the owner, excels at chess; take time to challenge him to a game.

The drive along the north shore is worth it to dine at **Toad Hall** (tel. 506/2692-8063, www.toadhallarenal.com, 8:30am-6pm daily), eight kilometers (5 miles) east of Nuevo

Arenal, where the ambience and lake views are sublime. Breakfast? Try a three-egg omelet or thick pancakes with fresh fruit ($7). Lunch? Perhaps a grilled chicken salad ($9) or fish taco ($10) washed down with a fresh fruit smoothie. Similar in style, **Restaurante Caballo Negro** (tel. 506/2694-4515, www.luckybugcr.net, 7am-8pm daily, $5-12), at Lucky Bug B&B, two kilometers (1.2 miles) west of Nuevo Arenal, offers an eclectic menu that includes schnitzel, chicken cordon bleu, eggplant parmigiana, and cappuccino. Dine overlooking a delightful garden and lake; you can even fish from a canoe and catch your own tilapia or bass. It has Wi-Fi.

For superb lake views, I head to the endearingly rustic **Café y Macadamia** (tel. 506/2692-2000, 7:30am-5pm daily), about six kilometers west of Nueva Arenal. The enthusiastic owners deliver tasty tilapia *campesina* ($10), beef chalupa ($9), and pasta tagliatelle ($9), plus macadamia muffins, blackberry cakes, and fruit shakes.

INFORMATION AND SERVICES

There's a **bank,** a **gas station,** and a **police station** (tel. 506/2694-4358) in Nuevo Arenal. **Lucky Bug Gallery** (tel. 506/2694-4515, www.luckybugcr.com), two kilometers (1.2 miles) west of Nuevo Arenal, and **Tom's Pan** (tel./fax 506/2694-4547), in the village of Nuevo Arenal, have Internet access.

GETTING THERE AND AROUND

Buses (Garaje Barquero, tel. 506/2232-5660) depart San José for Nuevo Arenal from Calle 16, Avenidas 1/3, at 6:15am, 8:40am, and 11:30am daily. Buses depart Cañas for Tilarán and Nuevo Arenal ($0.50) at 7:30am and 3pm daily; from Tilarán at 8am and 4:30pm daily; and from La Fortuna to Tilarán via Nuevo Arenal at 7am and 12:30pm daily.

An **express bus** departs Nuevo Arenal for San José via Ciudad Quesada at 2:45pm daily; additional buses depart for Ciudad Quesada at 8am and 2pm daily. A bus marked "Guatuso" also departs Arenal at 1:30pm daily for San Rafael, Caño Negro, and Upala in the northern lowlands.

Water taxis depart the dam at the east end of the lake and run to Nuevo Arenal, El Castillo, and Tronadora.

Los Chiles and Vicinity

LOS CHILES

Los Chiles, a small frontier town on the Río Frío, about 100 kilometers (60 miles) north of Ciudad Quesada and four kilometers (2.5 miles) south of the Nicaraguan border, is a gateway to Refugio Nacional de Vida Silvestre Caño Negro.

Los Chiles is reached by road via Muelle, an important crossroads village 21 kilometers (13 miles) north of Ciudad Quesada, at the junction of Highway 4 (running east-west between Upala and Puerto Viejo de Sarapiquí) and Highway 35 (north-south between Ciudad Quesada and Los Chiles). There's a gas station. Muelle is worth a visit to view the iguanas that reliably congregate in the treetops, seen at eye level from the bridge beside the Restaurante Iguana Azul.

The Reserva Biológica La Garza (tel. 506/2475-5222, www.hotellagarza.com) at Platanar, four kilometers (2.5 miles) south of the Muelle crossroads, protects wildlife on a 600-hectare (1,480-acre) working cattle and stud farm with forest trails. Horseback rides (from $10 for 90 minutes) and hikes are offered, and it has rappelling. Day visitors are welcome to use the pool and facilities.

The ruler-straight drive north from Muelle is modestly scenic, with the land rolling endlessly in a sea of lime-green pastures and citrus—those of the Ticofrut company, whose fincas stretch all the way to the Nicaraguan border. The colors are marvelous, the intense greens made more so by soils as red as lipstick. There are two civil-guard checkpoints on the road to Los Chiles.

Crossing into Nicaragua

As of 2014 it is possible to cross to or from Nicaragua at Tablillas, seven kilometers (4.5 miles) north of Los Chiles, and from there a new bridge crosses the Río San Juan and a new highway leads to Chontales in Nicaragua.

Foreigners can also cross into Nicaragua by a *colectivo* (shared water taxi, $10 pp) that departs Los Chiles for San Carlos de Nicaragua at 11am (it departs when full, which often isn't until 1:30pm) and 2:30pm daily. A private boat costs $150 for 5-7 passengers; call the public dock (tel. 506/2471-2277) or Río Frío Tours (tel. 506/2471-1090). The immigration office (tel. 506/2471-1233, 8am-6pm daily) is by the wharf.

Accommodations and Food

Los Chiles has only budget accommodations, most quite basic. The nicest place is Hotel Wilson Tulipán (tel./fax 506/2471-1414, www.hoteleswilson.com, $28 s, $41 d), opposite the immigration office, 50 meters (165 feet) from the dock. This clean, modern hotel features a pleasant country-style bar and restaurant. The 10 spacious, simply furnished air-conditioned rooms have private baths with hot water. There's secure parking, plus Wi-Fi, an Internet café, and a laundry; Óscar Rojas, the owner, arranges trips to Caño Negro.

Although billing itself as a convention hotel and social club for wealthy Ticos, American-run Tilajari Resort Hotel (tel. 506/2462-1212, www.tilajari.com, low season from $79 s/d, high season from $99 s/d), one kilometer (0.6 miles) west from the Muelle crossroads, is the best hotel for miles, with 76 spacious, nicely furnished air-conditioned rooms and junior suites, some with king beds; plus three tennis courts, a swimming pool, a children's pool, racquetball courts, a sauna, a gym, and a sensational whirlpool complex. There's an open-air riverside lounge bar, a disco, conference facilities, and the elegant Katira Restaurant, where chef Manuel Tuz conjures up gourmet nouvelle Costa Rican dishes. Ticos flock here on weekends. Crocodiles sun themselves on the banks of the Río San Carlos in plain view of guests, iguanas roost in the treetops, and hummingbirds emblazon the 16-hectare (40-acre) garden.

Information and Services

There's a hospital (tel. 506/2471-2000) 500 meters (0.3 miles) south of town and a Red Cross clinic on the northwest side of the plaza in Los Chiles. The police station (tel. 506/2471-1183) is on the main road as you enter town, and there's another by the wharf. There's a bank on the northeast side of the soccer field. Hotel Rancho Tulipán (tel./fax 506/2471-1414, 6am-11pm daily) has an Internet café.

Getting There

You can charter flights to Los Chiles airstrip. Autotransportes San Carlos (tel. 506/2255-4318) buses depart San José ($3.50) from Calle 12, Avenidas 7/9, at 5:30am and 3pm daily; return buses depart at 5am and 3:30pm daily. Buses run between Ciudad Quesada and Los Chiles throughout the day.

There's a gas station one kilometer (0.6 miles) south of town, and another 22 kilometers (14 miles) south of Los Chiles at Pavón.

★ CAÑO NEGRO WILDLIFE REFUGE

Refugio Nacional de Vida Silvestre Caño Negro (www.sinac.go.cr), southwest of Los Chiles, is a tropical everglade teeming with wildlife. The 9,969-hectare (24,634-acre) reserve protects a lush lowland basin of knee-deep watery sloughs and marshes centered on Lago Caño Negro, a seasonal lake fed by the fresh waters of the Río Frío. The region floods in wet season. In February-April, the area is reduced to shrunken lagoons; wildlife congregates along the watercourses, where caimans gnash and slosh out pools in the muck.

Caño Negro is a bird-watcher's paradise. The reserve protects the largest colony of neotropic cormorants in Costa Rica and the only permanent colony of Nicaraguan grackles. Cattle egrets, wood storks, anhingas, roseate spoonbills, and other waterfowl gather in the thousands. The reserve is also remarkable for its large population of caimans. Looking down into waters as black as Costa Rican coffee, you may see the dim forms of big snook,

male green iguana in orange mating color

silver-gold tarpon, and garish garfish. Bring plenty of insect repellent.

The hamlet of **Caño Negro,** 23 kilometers (14 miles) southwest of Los Chiles, nestles on the northwest shore of Lago Caño Negro. Locals make their living from fishing and guiding. The **ranger station** (tel. 506/2471-1309, 8am-5pm daily) is 400 meters (0.25 miles) inland from the dock and 200 meters (660 feet) west of the soccer field.

Local volunteers operate the **Criadero de Tortugas** (tel. 506/2876-1181, 8am-4pm daily, free), west of the soccer field and where turtles are bred for release to the wild. The village also has a butterfly garden: **Mariposario La Reinita** (tel. 506/2471-1301, 8am-4pm daily, $4), with 16 species flitting about within nets.

Sports and Recreation

Caño Negro's waters boil with tarpon, snook, drum, *guapote, machaca,* and *mojarra.* Fishing season is July-March (no fishing is allowed Apr.-June); licenses ($30) are required, obtainable from the ranger station in the village or through the various fishing lodges.

Hotel de Campo (tel. 506/2471-1012) and **Natural Lodge Caño Negro** (tel. 506/2471-1426, www.canonegrolodge.com) have fishing packages and lagoon tours, and you can rent canoes and kayaks. You can hire guides and boats at the dock. Try Joel Sandoval (tel. 506/8823-4026), or Manuel Castro of **Pantanal Tours** (tel. 506/8825-0193, $50 for up to 4 people for 4 hours).

Accommodations and Food

You can stay overnight in the Caño Negro ranger station if space is available ($6 pp).

You'll need a sleeping bag and a mosquito net. It has cold showers. Meals cost $5.

The **Hotel de Campo** (tel. 506/2471-1012, www.hoteldecampo.com, $79 s, $95 d), in Caño Negro village, stands lakeside amid landscaped grounds with a citrus orchard. Sixteen handsome, cross-ventilated, air-conditioned cabins have a choice of king or queen beds and have terra-cotta floors, lofty wooden ceilings with fans, and large modern baths with hot water. There's a bar and restaurant, a gift store, a tackle shop, and a swimming pool.

Fishing writer Jerry Ruhlow calls **Bar y Restaurante El Caimán** (tel. 506/2469-8200, 6:30am-7pm daily) "sort of a drive-in for boats." This unlikely find is beside the bridge at San Emilio; water vessels stop alongside it to order meals or cold beverages. It serves typical Tico fare. Canoe and boat trips are offered ($70 for 2 hours).

Getting There

A road from El Parque, 10 kilometers (6 miles) south of Los Chiles, runs 10 kilometers (6 miles) west to a bridge at San Emilio, from where you can reach Caño Negro village via a dirt road that continues south to Colonia Puntarenas, on the main La Fortuna-Upala road (Hwy. 4). A 4WD vehicle is recommended. Several companies in La Fortuna offer trips. **Canoa Aventura** (tel. 506/2479-8200, www.canoa-aventura.com) specializes in trips to Caño Negro.

Buses depart daily from Upala to Caño Negro village via Colonia Puntarenas at 11am and 3pm daily. You can rent a **boat** in Los Chiles ($70 for 2 people, $15 pp for 6 people or more).

Highway 4 to Upala

The mostly paved Carretera 4 (Hwy. 4) between La Fortuna (or, more precisely, Tanque, a major crossroads community eight kilometers/five miles east of La Fortuna) and Upala, has opened the extreme northwest of the Northern Zone as a new tourism frontier focused on the natural delights of Parque Nacional Volcán Tenorio.

Beyond Upala, the unpaved road leads via the community of San José to the hamlets of Brasilia and Santa Cecilia and, from there, by paved road to La Cruz, on the Pan-American Highway in the extreme northwest of Costa Rica.

SAN RAFAEL AND VICINITY

From Tanque, the highway shoots northwest to **San Rafael de Guatuso,** an agricultural town on the Río Frío, 40 kilometers (25 miles) northwest of Tanque. San Rafael (often called Guatuso) subsists largely on cattle ranching and rice farming. You can rent boats and guides here for trips down the Río Frío to the Caño Negro wildlife refuge, reached via dirt road from **Colonia Puntarenas,** 25 kilometers (16 miles) northwest of San Rafael.

Venado Caverns

At Jicarito, about 25 kilometers (16 miles) northwest of Tanque and 15 kilometers (9.5 miles) southeast of San Rafael de Guatuso, a paved road leads south seven kilometers (4.5 miles) to the mountain hamlet of Venado, nestled in a valley bottom and famous for the **Cavernas de Venado** (tel. 506/2478-9081 or 506/2478-8008, 9am-4pm daily, adults $22, children $12) two kilometers (1.2 miles) farther west. The limestone caverns, which extend 2,700 meters (8,860 feet) and feature stalactites, stalagmites, and underground streams, weren't discovered until 1945, when the owner of the farm fell into the hole. A guide will lead you on a two-hour exploration.

The admission cost includes use of a flashlight, a safety helmet, and rubber boots. Bats and tiny colorless frogs and fish inhabit the caves, which also contain seashell fossils and a luminous "shrine." Expect to get soaked—you'll wade up to your chest!—and covered with ooze (bring a change of clothes). The farm has a rustic *soda,* a swimming pool, and changing rooms with showers.

You can also reach Venado via a rough dirt road from the north shore of Laguna de Arenal. Tour operators in La Fortuna offer tours, as does **Cavernas de Venado Tours** (tel. 506/8344-2246, www.cavernasdevenado. com). A bus departs Ciudad Quesada for Venado at 1pm daily; it returns at 4pm.

Malekú Indigenous Reserve

Two kilometers (1.2 miles) east of San Rafael, a dirt road leads south to the 3,244-hectare (8,016-acre) **Reserva Indígena Malekú** (Malekú Indigenous Reserve, www.indigenasmalekus.com), in the foothills of the cordillera. Here, the **Centro Ecológico Malekú Araraf** (tel. 506/8888-4250, centroecologicomalekuararaf@yahoo.es, 8am-4pm daily) has trails and a cultural presentation. Competing **Eco-Adventure Tafa Malekú** (tel. 506/2464-0443, 7am-4pm daily, $1) has a museum on indigenous culture. **Rancho Típico Malekú Araraf** (tel. 506/8839-0540) has a traditional music and dance performance (by reservation only, $35 pp, including a tour). The three indigenous communities are gracious in the extreme—these lovely people, who speak Malekú Jaica, helped me immensely when I seriously injured myself falling through a rotten bridge.

Rustic Pathways (U.S. tel. 440-975-9691 or 800-321-4353, www.rusticpathways. com) offers a volunteer and study program for schoolchildren and students where you can contribute to and learn from the Malekú people.

The Malekú Culture

About 600 Malekú people survive on the Tongibe reservation (*palenque*) on the plains at the foot of Volcán Tenorio, near San Rafael de Guatuso, on land ceded to them by the government in the 1960s. While struggling to preserve their cultural identity, today they are mostly farmers who grow corn and a type of root called *tiquisqui*.

Until a few generations ago, Malekú (also known as Guatusos) strolled through San Rafael wearing clothes made of cured tree bark called *tana*. No one wears *tana* these days, but the Malekú take great pride in their heritage. Many continue to speak their own language. Radio Cultural Malekú (1580 AM, 88.3 FM) airs programs and announcements in Malekú, and Eliécer Velas Álvarez instructs the youngsters in Malekú at the elementary school in Tongibe.

The San Rafael area has many ancient tombs, and jade arrowheads and other age-old artifacts are constantly being dug up. Reconstructions of a typical Malekú village have been erected at Reserva Indígena Malekú and at Arenal Mundo Aventura, just south of La Fortuna.

Accommodations and Food

Nature Nirvana! That's **Leaves and Lizards** (tel. 506/2478-0023, U.S. tel. 888-828-9245, www.leavesandlizards.com, low season from $175 s/d, high season from $195 s/d, including breakfast), in the hills of Monterrey de Santo Domingo, 18 kilometers (11 miles) northwest of Tanque and three kilometers (2 miles) south of Highway 4. Run by Steve and Debbie Legg, an eco- and community-friendly couple from Florida, it has six simply furnished but delightful hillside cabins with decks for enjoying volcano views over 11 hectares (26 acres) of property. Meals are provided at the main lodge, which has Wi-Fi. Cabins have iPod docks, coffeemakers, and microwaves. A minimum three-night stay is required.

Getting There

Buses (tel. 506/2256-8914) for San Rafael de Guatuso depart San José ($4) from Calle 12, Avenidas 7/9, at 5am, 8:40am, and 11:30am daily. Buses also depart for San Rafael from Tilarán at noon daily.

TENORIO VOLCANO AND VICINITY

Upala, 40 kilometers (25 miles) northwest of San Rafael de Guatuso, is an agricultural town only 10 kilometers (6 miles) south of the Nicaraguan border. Dirt roads lead north to Lago de Nicaragua. From Upala, a paved road

leads south via the saddle between the Tenorio and Miravalles volcanoes before descending to the Pan-American Highway in Guanacaste. The only town is **Bijagua,** a center for cheese-making (and, increasingly, for ecotourism) 38 kilometers (24 miles) north of Cañas, on the northwest flank of Volcán Tenorio.

Several private reserves abut Parque Nacional Volcán Tenorio and grant access via trails. For example, about 200 meters (660 feet) north of the park access road, a dirt road leads to the American-owned **La Carolina Lodge** (tel. 506/2466-6393, www.lacarolinalodge.com), a ranch and stables with trails for horseback rides into the park. Another dirt road leads east from the Banco Nacional in Bijagua two kilometers (1.2 miles) to **Albergue Heliconia Lodge & Rainforest** (tel. 506/2466-8483, www.heliconiaslodge.com), run by a local cooperative. The lodge sits at 700 meters (2,300 feet) elevation, abutting the park. Three trails lead into prime rainforest and cloud forest.

★ Tenorio Volcano National Park

Volcán Tenorio (1,916 meters/6,286 feet), rising southeast of Upala, is blanketed in montane rainforest and protected within 18,402-hectare (45,472-acre) **Parque Nacional Volcán Tenorio** (www.sinac.go.cr, $10, via the private reserves $1). Local hiking is superb, albeit often hard going on higher slopes. Cougars and jaguars tread the forests, where birds and beasts abound.

A rugged dirt road (4WD vehicle required) that begins five kilometers (3 miles) north of Bijagua, on the west side of Tenorio, leads 11 kilometers (7 miles) to the main park entrance at the **Puesto El Pilón ranger station** (tel. 506/2200-0135).

Three trails are open to the public. The main trail—Sendero Misterio del Tenorio—leads 3.5 kilometers (2 miles) to the Río Celeste and **Los Chorros** hot springs; this is the only place where swimming is permitted. Set amid huge boulders, the springs change gradually, from near boiling close to the trail to pleasantly cool near the river. The second trail leads to the **Catarata del Río Celeste** (Río Celeste Waterfall) and the **Pozo Azul,** a teal-blue lagoon. A third trail, accessible with a guide only, leads to three waterfalls. You cannot hike to the summit (where tapirs drink at **Lago Las Dantas,** Tapir Lake, which fills the volcanic crater); access is permitted solely to biologists.

Guided hikes are offered by the local guides association: try **Jonathon Ramírez** (tel. 506/2402-1330, from $20). The ranger station has a small butterfly and insect exhibit, plus horseback riding. No camping is permitted within the park.

Accommodations and Food

There are several backpacker and simple budget accommodations in Upala and Bijagua.

Set high on the mountainside, **Albergue Heliconias** (tel. 506/2466-8483, www.heliconiaslodge.com, rooms $70 s, $85 d, cottages $85 s, $95 d, including breakfast) is the simplest of the eco-lodges; it's signed in town. It has six no-frills rustic cabins (two have a double bed and a bunk; four have two bunks) with small baths and hot showers, and there are four more upscale octagonal cottages. Dining is family style.

Feeling very much like the horse ranch that it is, **La Carolina Lodge** (tel. 506/2466-6393, www.lacarolinalodge.com, low season $90-105 s, $130-170 d, high season $100-115 s, $150-190 d, including 3 meals and a guided tour) occupies a charming farmstead on the north flank of Tenorio. It has four double rooms with solar-powered electricity and shared baths with hot water. There are also four private cabins with private baths. A wooden deck hangs over a natural river-fed pool, and a porch has rockers and hammocks. Rates include guided hikes and horseback riding.

The elegant hillside **Tenorio Lodge** (tel. 506/2466-8282, www.tenoriolodge.com, $115 s, $123 d), one kilometer south of Bijagua, offers great valley views from amid heliconia gardens. Its eight peak-roofed stylishly contemporary wooden bungalows have walls of glass, sponge-washed walls, glazed concrete floors, plus king beds, ceiling fans, and chic solar-powered designer baths. The glass-walled volcano-view restaurant (open to non-guests 7am-9pm daily for continental fare) is a class act and features live marimba music. At night, you can soak in either of two cedar hot tubs.

Avant-garde defines the French-run eco-conscious ★ **Celeste Mountain Lodge** (tel. 506/2278-6628, www.celestemountainlodge.com, $133 s, $168 d, including all meals and tax), enjoying a pristine and sensational location three kilometers (2 miles) northeast of Bijagua. Innovative and stylishly contemporary with its open-plan design, stone tile floor, gun-metal framework, glistening hardwood ceiling, and halogen lighting, this dramatic two-tier lodge boasts vast angled walls of glass plus glassless walls with panoramic volcano views from the restaurant and public areas. The 18 rooms, though small, are comfy, with king beds, lively fabrics, and stylish baths. Dining is gourmet (dishes here are "Tico fusion") and family-style. There's a wood-heated hot tub. Trails even accommodate disabled visitors, thanks to an innovative human-powered one-wheel rickshaw; packed lunches are prepared. I love this place, where everything is made of recycled materials, right down to biodegradable soaps.

A stunner by any standard, the non-smoking ★ **Río Celeste Hideaway** (tel. 506/2206-4000, www.riocelestehideaway. com, $190-259 s/d, includes breakfast), eight miles east of the entrance to Tenorio Volcano National Park, features gorgeous tropical architecture with dark hardwoods and rich Asian-inspired fabrics. Set in lush gardens, its 26 bungalows offer a king or two queen beds, luxurious linens, flat-screen TVs, iPod stations, CD/DVD players, private patios, and open-air showers. A free-form pool has a bar, and the Kantala Restaurant and blue-backlit Delirio bar are a dramatic space for enjoying cocktails and gourmet dishes.

Information and Services

A good resource for updates on this fast-evolving region is the **Cámara de Turismo Tenorio-Miravalles** (tel. 506/2466-7010, tenorio-miravalles@hotmail.com, 9am-3pm daily), the local Chamber of Tourism, on the south side of Bijagua.

There's a **hospital** (tel. 506/2470-0058) in Upala, plus a **bank** five blocks north of the bridge in Upala. The **police station** (Guardia Rural, tel. 506/2470-0134) is 100 meters (330 feet) north and west of the bridge.

Getting There

Buses (tel. 506/2221-3318 or 506/2470-0743) for Upala depart San José from Calle 12, Avenidas 3/5, four times daily 10:15am-7:30pm. Return buses depart Upala four times daily 4:30am-9:30pm. Buses also run between Cañas and Upala several times daily.

Puerto Viejo de Sarapiquí and Vicinity

The Llanura de San Carlos is the easternmost (and broadest) part of the northern lowlands. The Ríos San Carlos, Sarapiquí, and others snake across the landscape, vast sections of which are waterlogged for much of the year. The region today is dependent on the banana and pineapple industry, which has planted much of the land and woven a grid-work maze of dirt roads and railroad tracks linking towns.

Fortunately, swaths of rainforest still stretch north to the Río San Juan, linking Parque Nacional Braulio Carrillo with the rainforests of the Nicaraguan lowlands, much of which is protected within private reserves. Fishing is good, and there are crocodiles, river otters, and plenty of other wildlife to see while traveling on the rivers. Even manatees have been seen in the lagoons between the Río San Carlos and Río Sarapiquí.

There are two **routes to Puerto Viejo** from San José, forming a loop around Parque Nacional Braulio Carrillo. Both routes (western and eastern) over the mountains are subject to severe landslides.

PUERTO VIEJO DE SARAPIQUÍ

Puerto Viejo de Sarapiquís (not to be confused with Puerto Viejo de Talamanca, on the Caribbean coast), at the confluence of the Ríos Puerto Viejo and Sarapiquí, was Costa Rica's main shipping port in colonial times. It is still the main town in the region, with banks, a hospital, and other key services. Today, the local economy is dominated by banana and pineapples plantations, which stretch for miles around: You can take a tour of Dole's **Bananero La Colonia** (tel. 506/2768-8683 or 506/8383-4596, www.bananatourcostarica. com, $25), five kilometers (3 miles) southeast of Puerto Viejo, at 1:30pm Tuesday by appointment.

Accommodations and Food

The best option in Puerto Viejo is the simply furnished **Hotel Bambú** (tel. 506/2766-6005, www.elbambu.com, low season $65-74 s, $70-84 d, high season $72-82 s, $78-93 d, including breakfast), facing the soccer field. It has 40 clean, modern rooms with ceiling fans

Puerto Viejo de Sarapiquí and Vicinity

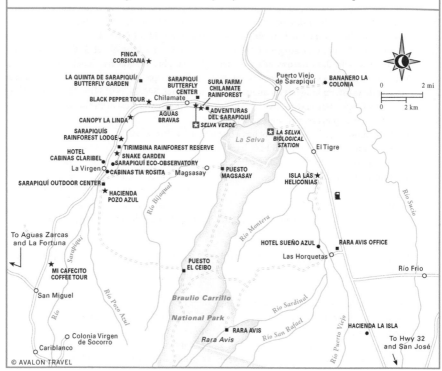

© AVALON TRAVEL

and air-conditioning, TVs, and hot water. It also has two self-sufficient apartments for six people, plus a large modern restaurant and a swimming pool in a thatch-fringed courtyard.

Information and Services

There are two banks near the soccer field. The **post office** is opposite Banco Nacional at the east end of Puerto Viejo. The **Red Cross** (tel. 506/2766-6212) adjoins the **police station** (tel. 506/2766-6575) at the west end of town, near the **hospital** (tel. 506/2766-6212).

Cafenet de Sarapiquí (tel. 506/2766-6223, 8am-10pm daily), at the west end of town, offers Internet access.

Getting There

Empresario Guapileños (tel. 506/2222-2727 or 506/2257-6859) buses depart the Gran Terminal Caribe in San José (2 hours, $2) 10 times 6:30am-6:30pm daily via the Guápiles Highway and Horquetas (do not take the Puerto Viejo de Talamanca bus—you want Puerto Viejo de Sarapiquís). **Taxis** wait on the north side of the soccer field, next to the bus stop, in Puerto Viejo.

WESTERN ROUTE VIA LA VIRGEN AND CHILAMATE

The less-trafficked western route to Puerto Viejo is via Vara Blanca, through the saddle of the Poás and Barva volcanoes, then dropping down to San Miguel (the junction westward for La Fortuna) and connecting to Puerto Viejo de Sarapiquís via La Virgen and Chilamate.

About 10 kilometers (6 miles) north of San

Sharks in the Río San Juan

If you see a shark fin slicing the surface of the Río San Juan, you will be forgiven for thinking you've come down with heatstroke. In fact, there *are* sharks in this freshwater river. The creatures, along with other species normally associated with salt water, migrate between the Atlantic Ocean and the murky waters of Lago de Nicaragua, navigating 169 kilometers (105 miles) of river and rapids en route. The sharks are classified as euryhaline species—they can cross from salt water to freshwater and back again with no ill effects.

For centuries, scientists were confounded by the sharks' presence in Lago de Nicaragua. The lake is separated from the Pacific by a 17-kilometer (11-mile) chunk of land, and since rapids on the Río San Juan seemingly prevent large fish from passing easily from the Caribbean, surely, the thinking went, the lake must have once been connected to one or the other ocean. Uplift of the Central American isthmus must have trapped the sharks in the lake.

Studies in the early 1960s, however, showed that there were no marine sediments on the lake bottom; thus the lake was never part of the Atlantic or the Pacific. It was actually formed when a huge block of land dropped between two fault lines; the depression then filled with water.

Then, ichthyologists decided to tag sharks with electronic tracking devices. It wasn't long before sharks tagged in the Caribbean turned up in Lago de Nicaragua, and vice versa. Incredibly, the sharks are indeed able to negotiate the rapids and move between lake and sea.

Miguel, the hamlet of La Virgen is the setting for several nature-related sites of interest, including the **Snake Garden** (tel. 506/2761-1059, snakegarden1@costarricense.co.cr, 9am-5pm daily, adults $15, students and children $10), which exhibits some 70 species of snakes, plus iguanas, turtles, and other reptiles. It also has night tours.

Hacienda Pozo Azul (tel. 506/2438-2616, U.S. tel. 877-810-6903, www.pozoazul.com), at La Virgen, raises Holstein cattle and doubles as an activity center offering horseback rides ($42-50), white-water trips ($58-84), a canopy tour ($53), river-canyon rappelling (from $40), and guided hikes ($27). A full-day, all-activity program costs $110, including transfers from San José.

Finca Corsicana (tel. 506/2761-1052, www.collinstreet.com/pages/finca_corsicana_home) offers two-hour tours of its organic pineapple farm (8am, 10am, noon, and 2pm daily, $15) at Llano Grande, seven kilometers (4.5 miles) northwest of La Virgen. It claims to be the largest such farm in the world.

Sarapiquí Eco-Observatory

Photographing birds is like shooting fish in a barrel at **Sarapiquí Eco-Observatory** (tel. 506/2761-0801 or 506/8346-7088, www.sarapiquieco-observatory.com, 7am-5pm daily, self-guided tour $20 adults, $10 children), a lodge at the edge of the Tirimbina Rainforest Reserve at La Virgen de Sarapiquí. Dedicated to birding, the lodge has a long shaded balcony and a second observation deck set up with scopes and feeders. Trails lead down through the rainforest to the river. Your bilingual host, David Lando Ramírez, is a font of knowledge, and a resident professional photographer offers photography workshops. Guided tours ($30) include nighttime walks. Tree-planting ($30) is a popular activity, as David and his dad also have a reforestation project with four types of habitats.

Sarapiquís Rainforest Lodge

Sarapiquís Rainforest Lodge (tel. 506/2761-1004, www.sarapiquis.com), formerly Centro Neotrópico Sarapiquís, on the banks of Río Sarapiquí about one kilometer (0.6 miles) north of La Virgen, is sponsored by the Belgian nonprofit Landscape Foundation and serves as a scientific research and educational center as well as an eco-lodge.

The **Museum of Indigenous Culture** (9am-5pm daily), with more than 400 pre-Columbian artifacts and a 60-seat movie theater, is a focal point of the center. There's an archaeological dig—**Alma Alta Archaeological Park**—of four indigenous tombs dating from 800 BC to AD 155, plus a reconstruction of an indigenous village. A farm grows fruits and vegetables based on ecological farming practices. There's an astronomical observatory, and you can wander the trails though **Chester's Field Botanical Garden,** with about 500 native species.

Visitors are welcomed on either of two mandatory tours led by indigenous guides ($15-20), providing an in-depth insight into Costa Rica's indigenous culture, including a display of pottery-making.

Tirimbina Rainforest Reserve

A 250-meter-long (820-foot-long) canopied bridge leads across the river gorge and into the **Tirimbina Rainforest Reserve** (tel. 506/2761-0333, www.tirimbina.org, 7am-5pm daily), adjoining Sarapiquís Rainforest Lodge. It has eight kilometers (5 miles) of trails, with suspension bridges and a 110-meter (360-foot) canopy walkway. A museum portrays life in the forest. Nature walks cost $15 self-guided, $25 guided, and there's also a World of Bats night walk ($22), a chocolate tour ($27), and bird-watching ($25). Students and children get discounts. Tirimbina hosts researchers and offers accommodations, from bunk rooms to private air-conditioned rooms.

★ Selva Verde

Selva Verde (tel. 506/2761-1800, U.S. tel. 800-451-7111, www.selvaverde.com, 7am-3pm daily, $5, free to hotel guests), on the banks of the Río Sarapiquí, about one kilometer (0.6 miles) east of Chilamate and eight kilometers (5 miles) west of Puerto Viejo, is a private reserve protecting some 192 hectares (474 acres) of primary rainforest adjacent to Parque Nacional Braulio Carrillo. At its heart is an internationally acclaimed nature lodge and the **Sarapiquí Conservation Learning Center** (Centro de Enseñanza), with a lecture room and a library. The reserve is renowned

for its birdlife, and it has a small butterfly garden. Trails lead through the forests (poison dart frogs abound), and the lodge has naturalist guides. Guided hiking is available (2 hours adults $22, children $11), including by night (adults $20, children $10), plus the reserve offers a wildlife boat ride (adults $30, children $15).

Recreation

The area is popular for waterborne nature-viewing or fishing trips on the Río Sarapiquí, as well as white-water rafting and kayaking. The most popular put-in point is at La Virgen, with Class II and III rapids below. A second put-in point is Chilamate, offering more gentle Class I and II floats. Companies that offer tours include **Costa Rica Expeditions** (tel. 506/2257-0766, www.costaricaexpeditions. com) and **Ríos Tropicales** (tel. 506/2233-6455, www.riostropicales.com). **Aguas Bravas** (tel. 506/2766-6524 or 506/2296-2072, www.aguasbravascr.com), at Chilamate, also specializes in white-water trips ($60) and has bird-watching tours, horseback riding, and other adventures.

You can explore the rainforest canopy at the **Sarapiquí Canopy Tour** (tel. 506/2290-6015, www.crfunadventures.com), which has 15 platforms, a suspension bridge, and one kilometer (0.6 miles) of zip line. It has a full-day nature-viewing river trip and canopy tour combo ($95).

Accommodations

Want to really feel as one with nature? **Hacienda Pozo Azul** (tel. 506/2761-1360, www.pozoazul.com, $80 s, $92 d, including breakfast), at La Virgen, makes it easy with its 30 roomy four-person tent-suites under tarps on raised platforms in the forest. Clean, well-maintained shared baths have hot water. There's even Wi-Fi. The hacienda also has **Magasay Jungle Lodge** ($60 s, $96 d, including all meals), bordering Parque Nacional Braulio Carrillo. This wooden lodge has 10 rooms with bunks, plus solar power and hot showers.

Perfect for birders, ★ **Selva Verde** (tel. 506/2766-6800, U.S. tel. 800-451-7111, www. selvaverde.com, low season $99-142 s, $117-205 d, high season $116-165 s, $134-225 d, including breakfast) has a 45-room lodge set in eight hectares (20 acres) of lush gardens and forest on the banks of the Río Sarapiquí, about one kilometer (0.6 miles) east of Chilamate. Thatched walkways lead between the spacious and airy hardwood cabins raised on stilts. Choose cabins with private baths at the River Lodge, or rooms with shared baths at the Creek Lodge; all are simply furnished and have ceiling fans, two single beds, screened windows, large baths with piping-hot water, and verandas with hammocks and rockers. Five more upscale bungalow rooms are air-conditioned. There's a swimming pool, and meals are served buffet-style. Selva Verde is popular with groups; book well in advance.

The **Sarapiquí Rainforest Lodge** (tel. 506/2761-1004, U.S./Canada tel. 866-581-0782, www.sarapiquis.org, $105 s/d year-round), one kilometer (0.6 miles) north of La Virgen, is centered on a thatched eco-lodge in pleasing ocher yellow and sienna. Each of three units has eight "deluxe" rooms shaped like pie slices arrayed in a circle around an atrium. There are 16 rooms in an adjunct wing. All feature lively fabrics, handmade furniture, natural stone floors, fans, large walk-in showers, and Wi-Fi. Eight rooms are air-conditioned. Although they lack windows, a glass door opens to a wraparound veranda overlooking the gardens or river. There's a splendid restaurant.

Food

If traveling the Vara Blanca-San Miguel route, do stop at **Soda Galería de Colibrí** (7am-5pm daily), which is all that remains of the former village of Cinchona, destroyed by the 2009 earthquake. The owner lost his entire family yet clings on. His simple *soda* serves typical Costa Rican dishes, including *cuajada,* homemade cheese in a tortilla wrap.

The restaurant at **Selva Verde** (7am-8pm daily, $10-15), about one kilometer (0.6 miles)

east of Chilamate, is open to nonguests, so pop in for filling and tasty home-style Costa Rican cooking. The elegant **El Sereno Restaurant** (7am-10pm daily), at Centro Neotrópico Sarapiquís, one kilometer (0.6 miles) north of La Virgen, offers gourmet dining.

Getting There

Buses (tel. 506/2257-6859) depart the Gran Terminal Caribe in San José 10 times 6:30am-6:30pm daily, via Puerto Viejo de Sarapiquí. Buses also connect San Miguel to La Fortuna.

EASTERN ROUTE VIA EL CRUCE AND HORQUETAS

The heavily trafficked eastern route between San José and Puerto Viejo de Sarapiquí traverses the saddle between the Barva and Irazú volcanoes via **Highway 32** (Guápiles Hwy.), dropping down through Parque Nacional Braulio Carrillo and then north via Horquetas. At the base of the mountains, at **El Cruce,** is the junction with **Highway 4,** which runs due north for 34 kilometers (21 miles) to Puerto Viejo.

The only village between El Cruce and Puerto Viejo is **Horquetas,** exactly midway between the two. Horquetas is home to the **Jardín Ecológico Pierella** (tel. 506/8752-9154, www.pierella.com, by appointment, $15), a butterfly breeding center set in a manicured garden. Visitors also get to see animals such as peccaries, agoutis, and toucans. María Luz Jiménez gives a splendid 20-minute tour of her *palmito* plantation at **Palmitours** (tel. 506/2764-1495, tourpalmito@gmail.com, 9am-5pm daily, $35, including lunch), about five kilometers (3 miles) south of La Selva. Her roadside restaurant serves all things made of *palmito,* including a delicious lasagna, pancakes, ceviche, and muffins.

Isla Las Heliconias

Isla Las Heliconias (Heliconia Island, tel. 506/2764-5220, www.heliconiaisland.com, self-guided tour $12, guided tour $18), about five kilometers (3 miles) north of Horquetas, is indeed an island-turned-heliconia garden, created with an artist's eye and lovingly tended by naturalist Tim Ryan and now tended by Dutch owners Henk and Carolien Peters-van Duijnhoven. The exquisite garden was started in 1992 and today boasts about 80 species of heliconia, plus ginger and other plants, shaded by almond trees in which green macaws nest. The garden also includes palms, orchids, and bamboo from around the world. Needless to say, birds abound.

Nearby, **Frog's Heaven** (tel. 506/8891-8589, 8am-8pm daily, $35) is another tropical garden, this one a habitat for two dozen or so frog species to hop around or be discovered hiding beneath a leaf. Guided tours are offered by owner José.

Rara Avis

Rara Avis (tel. 506/2764-1111, www.rara-avis.com), a 1,280-hectare (3,163-acre) rainforest reserve abutting Parque Nacional Braulio Carrillo, 15 kilometers (9.5 miles) west of Horquetas, is one of the original sustainable projects in the country. It hosts a biological research station and several novel projects designed to show that a rainforest can be economically viable if left intact, not cut down. Projects include ecotourism and producing

exportable orchids and philodendrons for wicker. There's a butterfly farm and an orchid garden. More than 360 bird species inhabit the reserve, along with jaguars, tapirs, monkeys, anteaters, coatimundis, and butterflies galore.

Visitors can view the canopy from two platforms ($35, including 2-hour guided hike), including one at the foot of a spectacular double waterfall: Rara Avis gets up to 550 centimeters (217 inches) of rain per year and has no dry months. The trails range from easy to difficult. Rubber boots are recommended (the lodge has boots to lend for those with U.S. shoe sizes 12 or smaller). Guided walks include night tours ($15).

Most people consider the experience of getting to Rara Avis part of the fun; others have stated that no reward is worth three hours of bumping around on the back of a canopied tractor-pulled trailer. Even the tractor (which leaves Horquetas at 9am) sometimes gets stuck. Rara Avis is not a place for a day visit, and a two-night minimum stay is required.

Rara Avis has two accommodations options. **Waterfall Lodge** ($84 s, $160 d) features eight rooms, each with a private bathtub with hot water and a wraparound balcony with great views. You can also opt for one of four simple two-room cabins with bunks ($70

welcome sign at Isla Las Heliconias, near Horquetas

Following the Great Green Macaw

The **Bird Route** (www.costaricanbirdroute.com), launched in 2010 to promote ecotourism, offers four bird-watching itineraries centered on 15 nature reserves that together are home to more than 500 bird species. The reserves encompass a wide range of habitats. The prime focus is on the Sarapiquí-San Carlos region, centered on Puerto Viejo de Sarapiquí and Los Chiles. This is one of the last remaining habitats of the endangered great green macaw (one of the four itineraries is called "On the Trail of the Great Green Macaw"). The idea behind this is to promote bird-watching as a stimulus to conserve bird habitat, not least by providing income for local landowners and communities. You can purchase a map ($13) online and explore on your own, but I highly recommend hiring a guide, which you can also book online.

s, $150 d). Reservations are essential. Rates include meals.

★ La Selva Biological Station

One of Costa Rica's premier birding sites, **Estación Biológica La Selva** (tel. 506/2766-6565, www.ots.ac.cr), four kilometers (2.5 miles) south of Puerto Viejo, is a biological research station run by the Organization of Tropical Studies (OTS). The station is centered on a 1,500-hectare (3,700-acre) reserve—mostly premontane rainforest but with varied habitats—linked to the northern extension of Parque Nacional Braulio Carrillo. More than 420 bird species have been identified here, as have more than 500 species of butterflies, 120 species of mammals, and 55 species of snakes. The arboretum displays more than 1,000 tree species.

Almost 60 kilometers (37 miles) of trails snake through the reserve. Some have boardwalks; others are no more than muddy pathways. Rubber boots or waterproof hiking boots are essential, as is rain gear. Guided nature walks ($30-40) are offered at 8am and 1:30pm daily, and an early-bird bird-watching tour ($30) departs at 5:30am. Visitors who overnight can take a nocturnal tour ($40). You cannot explore alone, and only 65 people at a time are allowed in the reserve; nonscientists are restricted to certain trails. Still, the wildlife viewing is phenomenal. On

Welcome to La Selva Biological Station.

two recent visits, I photographed peccaries almost within reach, plus saw lots of poison dart frogs, snakes, crocodiles, and several great curassows. It is often booked solid months in advance. Reservations are required.

You can even overnight in comfortable dormitory-style accommodations (reservations c/o OTS, tel. 506/2524-0627, $98 s, $194 d, including meals, tax, and guided hike) with four bunks per room and communal baths; some are wheelchair-accessible. Meals are served right on time, and latecomers get the crumbs.

The OTS operates a shuttle van from San José ($10) on Monday, space permitting (researchers and students have priority), and between La Selva and Puerto Viejo Monday-Saturday. **Transporte Caribe** (tel. 506/2221-7990) buses from San José will drop you off at the entrance, from where you'll need to walk two kilometers (1.2 miles) to La Selva.

Accommodations and Food

Farm-style rusticity rules at **Hotel Sueño Azul** (tel. 506/2764-1000, www.suenoazulresort.com, $90-142 s/d year-round), two miles northwest of Horquetas. Rattan and bamboo features enhance the 55 simply appointed rooms; suites have outdoor whirlpool tubs. There's a lagoon and trails into the adjacent forest, plus horseback riding, a canopy tour, a rodeo, a folkloric evening, and even a full-service spa and yoga studio. The highlight, though, is a delightful rustic restaurant occupying a former cattle corral (7am-10pm daily), overlooking a free-form pool with a cascade. It's adorned with saddles and farm implements hanging from the dark wood-beamed ceiling; it serves *típico* dishes.

Belgian expat Jean-Pierre Knockeart plays congenial host at the 19-room ★ **Hacienda La Isla** (tel. 506/2764-2576, www.haciendalaisla.com, low season standard $109 s/d, suite $146 s/d, high season standard $126 s/d, suite $165 s/d, including tax), a boutique hotel three kilometers (2 miles) north of El Cruce. Themed to Costa Rica's colonial past, this former hacienda exudes the feel of yesteryear and is set amid orchards and lush gardens. The rooms and one suite are exquisitely furnished, with hardwood pieces and ocher color schemes. The restaurant delivers gourmet fusion cuisine. It has rainforest trails, and horseback riding is a specialty.

Getting There

Empresario Guapileños (tel. 506/2222-2727 or 506/2257-6859) buses depart the Gran Terminal Caribe in San José (2 hours, $2) 10

peccary at La Selva Biological Station

Whose River Is It?

Nicaragua has disputed Costa Rica's territorial rights to free use of the Río San Juan, while Costa Rica disputes Nicaragua's claim that the river is entirely Nicaraguan territory. The 205-kilometer-long (127-mile-long) river, which flows from Lago de Nicaragua to the Caribbean, marks most of the border between these countries. When you are on the water, you are inside Nicaragua.

Costa Ricans have had right of commercial use of the Río San Juan, but since 2001 Nicaraguan authorities have boarded Costa Rican boats and fined foreigners aboard ($25) for using the river without Nicaraguan visas. This has primarily affected sportfishing boats from Costa Rican lodges in Barra del Colorado, and tour boats and water taxis operating from Los Chiles.

In 2009 the International Court of Justice adjudicated on access rights to the river. Essentially it reaffirmed an 1858 treaty that acknowledged Nicaragua's ownership of the river while guaranteeing Costa Ricans free access. The important proviso was that non-Costa Rican passengers aboard Costa Rican vessels using the river are not required to obtain Nicaraguan visas. Both countries accepted the verdict, which also granted Nicaragua the right to build an interoceanic canal if it compensated Costa Rica for the damage. However, Costa Rica's militarized police force will no longer be permitted to patrol the river, which is also an avenue for drug trafficking. The two nations actually came to blows over this issue in 1998. The ruling paved the way for increased tourism along the river, which is bordered by the Refugio de Vida Silvestre Corredor Fronterizo (Frontier Corridor National Wildlife Refuge).

Just as the dust settled, in November 2010, Nicaragua's leftist president, Daniel Ortega, decided to fan the nationalist flames by accusing Costa Rica of wanting to seize the river. This came after Costa Rica appealed to the Organization of American States (OAS) to intervene after Nicaraguan dredging of the river intruded onto Isla Calero, in Costa Rican territory, and Nicaraguan troops occupied Costa Rican soil.

times 6:30am-6:30pm daily via the Guápiles Highway and Horquetas (do not take the Puerto Viejo de Talamanca bus—you want Puerto Viejo de Sarapiquís).

To get to Rara Avis in time, you will need to take the 6:30am bus from San José. This will drop you at Horquetas in time for the tractor-hauled transfer to Rara Avis from Horquetas at 9am daily. If driving, you can leave your car in a parking lot at the Rara Avis office in Horquetas. Later arrivals can rent horses ($35) for the four-hour ride, but not after 2pm.

FRONTIER CORRIDOR NATIONAL WILDLIFE REFUGE

The **Refugio Nacional de Vida Silvestre Corredor Fronterizo** (www.sinac.go.cr) extends for a width of two kilometers (1.2 miles) along the entire border with Nicaragua, coast to coast. Boats ply the Río San Juan, connecting Puerto Viejo de Sarapiquí with Barra del Colorado and Tortuguero (and west with San Carlos in Nicaragua). The nature-viewing is fantastic, with birds galore, monkeys and sloths in the trees along the riverbank, and crocodiles and caimans poking their nostrils and eyes above the water.

You can even visit **El Castillo de la Inmaculada Concepción,** built by the Spanish in 1675 on a hill dominating the river and intended to repel pirates and English invaders. The ruins are in Nicaragua, three kilometers (2 miles) west of where the Costa Rican border moves south of the river (you'll need your passport).

The transborder park was created in 1985, when Nicaraguan president Daniel Ortega seized on the idea as a way to demilitarize the area, at the time being used by anti-Sandinista rebels. Ortega proposed the region be declared an international park for peace and gave it the name Sí-a-Paz—Yes to Peace. Efforts by the Arias administration to kick the rebels out of Costa Rica's northern zone led to demilitarization of the area, but lack of funding and political difficulties prevented the two countries from making much progress. The end of the Nicaraguan war in 1990 allowed the governments to dedicate more money to the project, encompassing heavily logged and denuded terrain between the Ríos Sarapiquí and San Carlos and extending northward from Parque Nacional Braulio Carrillo to the Reserva Biológica Indio Maíz, which protects nearly 500,000 hectares (1.2 million acres) of rainforest in the southeast corner of Nicaragua.

In 2003 the efforts led to formalization of the boundaries of the 30,000-hectare (74,000-acre) **Refugio Nacional de Vida Silvestre Maquenque** (www.sinac.go.cr), a vast wildlife refuge that incorporates several disparate ecosystems and reserves linking the Corredor Fronterizo reserve with the Corredor Ecológico San Juan-La Selva (San Juan-La Selva Biological Corridor), covering 340,000 hectares (840,000 acres) and 29 protected areas, including Parque Nacional Tortuguero and the Barra del Colorado reserve.

Maquenque incorporates Humedal Lacustrino de Tamborcito, a wetland reserve that is prime habitat for manatees and tapirs; and **Laguna del Lagarto** (tel. 506/2289-8163, www.lagarto-lodge-costa-rica.com),

a private reserve that protects 500 hectares (1,240 acres) of virgin rainforest and bayou swamps harboring crocodiles, caimans, turtles, and poison dart frogs, along with ocelots, sloths, and all kinds of colorful bird species, including the rare green macaw. Laguna del Lagarto also has a butterfly garden, forest trails for hiking, and horseback rides ($20 for 2 hours). Four-hour boat trips on the San Carlos and San Juan Rivers cost $26 pp (minimum 4 people). It offers transfers from San José and can be reached by road via the hamlet of Boca Topada—the gateway—from Aguas Zarcasa.

Accommodations and Food

Perfect for nature lovers, the delightfully rustic **Laguna del Lagarto Lodge** (tel. 506/2289-8163, www.lagarto-lodge-costa-rica.com, low season $45 s, $60 d, high season $51 s, $75 d) offers 20 comfortable rooms in two buildings (18 with private baths, 2 with a shared bath, and all with hot water). Each has a large terrace with a view overlooking the Río San Carlos and the forest. A restaurant serves hearty Costa Rican buffet meals and arranges transfers.

A virtual clone, **Maquenque Eco-Lodge** (tel. 506/2479-8200, www.maquenqueecolodge.com, low season $91 s, $113 d,

water taxis on the Río Sarapiquí, at Puerto Viejo de Sarapiquí

high season $101 s, $125 d) also has delight- ful cabins overlooking a lagoon at the heart of its own 60-hectare (148-acre) reserve. It has eight kilometers (5 miles) of trails for hiking and horseback riding, plus canoe trips (www. canoa-aventura.com).

Information

The **Ministro de Ambiente y Energía** (Ministry of Environment and Energy, tel. 506/2471-2191, refugio.fronterizo@sinac.co.cr, 8am-4pm Wed. and Fri. only), in Los Chiles, has responsibility for administering the wild- life refuge; call or visit for information.

Getting There

A **water taxi** ($5) departs the dock in Puerto Viejo at 1:30pm for Trinidad (on the east bank of the Río Sarapiquí at its junction with the Río San Juan). Water taxis are also for hire, from slender motorized canoes to canopied tour boats for 8-20 passengers. Trips cost about $10 per hour for up to five people. A full-day trip to the Río San Juan and back costs from $100 per boat. Expect to pay $500 for a charter boat (for up to 20 people) all the way down the Río San Juan to Barra del Colorado and Tortuguero.

Oasis Nature Tours (tel. 506/2766-6260, www.oasisnaturetours.com) offers boat trips to El Castillo and into Nicaragua.

By road, Refugio Nacional de Vida Silvestre Maquenque can be reached via the agricultural town of Pital, about six kilo- meters (4 miles) northeast of Aguas Zarcas. A road leads due north from Pital via Boca Topada to Laguna del Lagarto. **Buses** (tel. 506/2258-8914) for Pital depart San José from Calle 12, Avenidas 7/9, four times daily 7:40am-7:30pm; and from Ciudad Quesada hourly 5:30am-9:30pm daily. From Pital, buses run to Boca Tapada at 9am and 4:30pm daily; return buses depart Pital at 5am and noon daily.

Guanacaste and the Northwest

Guanacaste has been called Costa Rica's Wild West. The name Guanacaste derives from *quahnacaztlan,* a word from an indigenous language meaning "place near the ear trees," for the tall and broad *guanacaste* (free ear or ear pod) tree that spreads its gnarled branches long and low to the ground; during the hot summer, all that walks, crawls, or flies gathers in its cool shade in the heat of midday.

The lowlands to the west are a vast alluvial plain of seasonally parched rolling hills broadening to the north and dominated by giant cattle ranches interspersed with smaller pockets of cultivation. To the east rises a mountain meniscus—the Cordillera de Guanacaste and Cordillera de Tilarán—studded with symmetrical volcanic cones spiced with bubbling mud pits and steaming vents. These mountains are lushly forested on their higher slopes. Rivers cascade down the flanks, slow to a meandering pace, and pour into the Tempisque basin, an unusually arid region smothered by dry forest and cut through by watery sloughs. The coast is indented with bays, peninsulas, and warm sandy beaches that are some of the least visited, least accessible, and yet most beautiful in the country. Sea turtles use many as nurseries.

The country's first national park, Santa Rosa, was established here, the first of more than a dozen national parks, wildlife refuges, and biological reserves in the region. The array of ecosystems in the region ranges from pristine shores to volcanic heights, encompassing just about every imaginable ecosystem within Costa Rica.

No region of Costa Rica displays its cultural heritage as overtly as Guanacaste, whose distinct flavor owes much to the blending of Spanish and indigenous Chorotega cultures. The people who today inhabit the province are tied to old bloodlines and live and work on the cusp between cultures. Today one can still see deeply bronzed wide-set faces and pockets of Chorotega life.

Costa Rica's national costume and music emanate from this region, as does the *punto guanacasteco,* the country's official dance.

Previous: colonial-era architecture, Puntarenas; Monteverde Cloud Forest Reserve. **Above:** three-toed sloth, Monteverde.

Look for ★ to find recommended
sights, activities, dining, and lodging.

Highlights

★ **Monteverde Cloud Forest:** This world-famous biological reserve is laced by fabulous nature trails for viewing quetzals and other wildlife (page 67).

★ **Jewels of the Rainforest Insect Museum:** This private insect collection is one of the nation's preeminent nature displays (page 72).

★ **The Bat Jungle:** Everything you learn about these amazing and ecologically imperative flying mammals will give you a whole new respect for them (page 73).

★ **Centro de Rescate Las Pumas:** At this rescue center, you're guaranteed eyeball-to-eyeball encounters with all the big cats you're unlikely to see in the wild (page 84).

★ **Río Corobicí:** A float trip on this relatively calm river is fun for the whole family (page 84).

★ **Las Hornillas Volcanic Activity Center:** This active walk-through crater has therapeutic mud pools you can actually bathe in (page 86).

★ **Río Perdido Activity Center:** This activity center on the lower slopes of Volcán Miravalles guarantees plenty of thrills, plus a sensational restaurant and spa (page 86).

★ **Palo Verde National Park:** Bird-watching par excellence is the name of the game at this watery world best explored by boat (page 87).

★ **Rincón de la Vieja National Park:** Magnificent scenery, bubbling mud pools, and trails to the volcano's summit are highlights of this national park (page 94).

★ **Santa Rosa National Park:** The finest of the dry-forest reserves offers unrivaled wildlife-viewing and top-notch surfing (page 98).

The region's heritage can still be traced in the creation of clay pottery and figurines. The campesino life here revolves around the ranch, and dark-skinned *sabaneros* (cowboys) are a common sight. Come fiesta time, nothing rouses so much cheer as the *corridas de toros* (bullfights) and *topes*, the region's colorful horse parades. Guanacastecans love a fiesta: The biggest occurs each July 25, when Guanacaste celebrates its independence from Nicaragua.

Guanacaste's climate is in contrast to the rest of the country. The province averages less than 162 centimeters (64 inches) of rain per year, though regional variation is extreme. For half the year (Nov.-Apr.) the plains receive no rain, it is hotter than Hades, and the sun beats down hard as a nail, although cool winds bearing down from northern latitudes can lower temperatures pleasantly along the coast December-February. The dry season usually lingers slightly longer than elsewhere in Costa Rica. The Tempisque basin is the country's driest region and receives less than 45 centimeters (18 inches) of rain in years of drought, mostly in a few torrential downpours during the six-month rainy season. The mountain slopes receive much more rain, noticeably on the eastern slopes, which are cloud-draped and deluged for much of the year.

PLANNING YOUR TIME

Guanacaste is a large region; its numerous attractions are spread out, and getting between any two major areas can eat up the better part of a day. The region is diverse enough to justify exploring it in its entirety, for which you should budget no less than one week. Monteverde alone requires a minimum of two days, and ideally three or four, to take advantage of all that it offers. Nor would you want to rush exploring Parque Nacional Rincón de la Vieja, requiring two or three nights.

The Pan-American Highway (Hwy. 1) cuts through the heart of lowland Guanacaste, ruler-straight almost all the way between the Nicaraguan border in the north and Puntarenas in the south. Juggernaut trucks frequent the fast-paced and potholed road, which since 2013 is now two lanes in both directions for most of its length. Drive cautiously! North of Liberia, the route is superbly scenic. Almost every sight of importance lies within a short distance of the highway, accessed by dirt side roads. If traveling by bus, sit on the east-facing side for the best views.

Touristy it might be, but Monteverde, the biggest draw, delivers in heaps. Its numerous attractions include canopy tours, horseback riding, and art galleries along with orchid, snake, frog, and butterfly exhibits, but most famous are its several cloud-forest reserves.

Recent years have seen a boost in regional tourism following expansion of the international airport at Liberia, now served with direct flights by most large U.S. carriers. The airport is well served by car rental companies. The town of Liberia is a gateway to both the Nicoya Peninsula and Parque Nacional Rincón de la Vieja, popular for hikes to the summit and for horseback rides and canopy tours from nature lodges outside the park. Liberia makes a good base for forays farther afield.

The Cámara de Turismo Guanacasteca (Guanacaste Chamber of Tourism, tel. 506/2690-9501, www.letsgoguanacaste.com), is a good resource.

Guanacaste and the Northwest

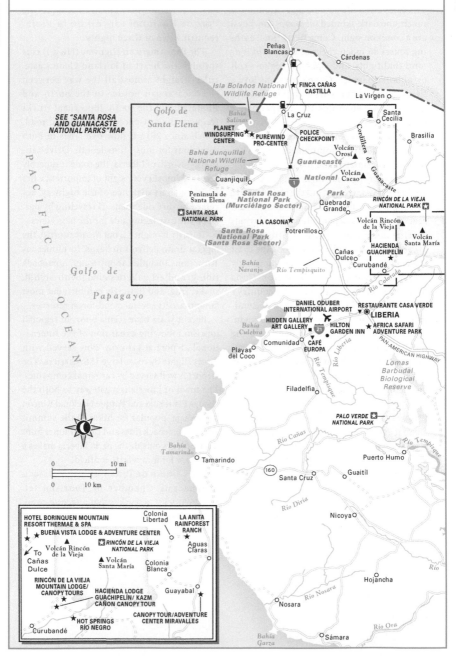

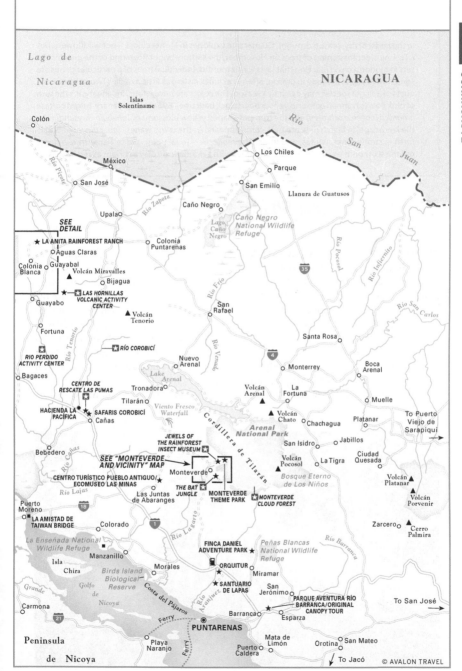

Lago de Nicaragua

Nicaragua

NICARAGUA

Islas Solentiname

Colón

Río San Juan

México

Los Chiles

Parque

San José

San Emilio

Llanura de Guatusos

Río Zapote

Caño Negro

Upala

Lago Caño Negro

Caño Negro National Wildlife Refuge

★ LA ANITA RAINFOREST RANCH

Aguas Claras

Colonia Puntarenas

Río Pocosol

Río Infiernito

35

Colonia Blanca

Guayabal

Volcán Miravalles ▲

Bijagua

Río Frío

Río San Carlos

Guayabo

★ ⬛ LAS HORNILLAS VOLCANIC ACTIVITY CENTER

San Rafael

▲ Volcán Tenorio

Fortuna

Río Tenorio

⬛ RÍO COROBICÍ

Santa Rosa

Río Venado

RÍO PERDIDO ACTIVITY CENTER ⬛

Nuevo Arenal

4

Monterrey

Boca Arenal

Bagaces

Lake Arenal

Volcán Arenal

La Fortuna

CENTRO DE RESCATE LAS PUMAS ⬛

Tronadora

Muelle

Tilarán

Viento Fresco Waterfall

▲ Volcán Chato

Chachagua

Platanar

To Puerto Viejo de Sarapiquí

HACIENDA LA PACÍFICA

★ SAFARIS COROBICÍ

Cañas

Cordillera de Tilarán

Arenal National Park

San Isidro

Jabillos

Ciudad Quesada

Bebedero

Río Cañas

JEWELS OF THE RAINFOREST INSECT MUSEUM ⬛

★★

Volcán Pocosol

La Tigra

SEE "MONTEVERDE AND VICINITY" MAP

Monteverde ★★

★

Bosque Eterno de Los Niños

Volcán Platanar ▲

CENTRO TURÍSTICO PUEBLO ANTIGUO/ ECOMUSEO LAS MINAS

Río Lajas

Las Juntas de Abaranges

THE BAT ⬛ JUNGLE

MONTEVERDE THEME PARK

⬛ MONTEVERDE CLOUD FOREST

Volcán Porvenir ▲

Puerto Moreno

16

Río Lagarto

Colorado

1

Zarcero

Cerro Palmira ▲

⬛■ LA AMISTAD DE TAIWAN BRIDGE

La Ensenada National Wildlife Refuge

Manzanillo

Morales

FINCA DANIEL ADVENTURE PARK ★

Peñas Blancas National Wildlife Refuge

Río Barranca

Isla Chira

Birds Island Biological Reserve

🏛 ORQUITUR

★ SANTUARIO DE LAPAS

Miramar

To San José

Golfo de Nicoya

Costa del Pájaros

Río Aranjuez

San Jerónimo

★ PARQUE AVENTURA RÍO BARRANCA/ORIGINAL CANOPY TOUR

Grande

Carmona

21

Ferry

Barranca

Esparza

Peninsula de Nicoya

Playa Naranjo

Ferry

◉ PUNTARENAS

Puerto Caldera

Mata de Limón

Orotina

San Mateo

To Jacó

© AVALON TRAVEL

A Palette in Bloom

In the midst of dry-season drought, Guanacaste explodes in Monet colors—not wildflowers, but a Technicolor blossoming of trees. In November, the saffron-bright flowering of the *guachipelín* sets in motion a chain reaction that lasts for six months. Individual trees of a particular genus are somehow keyed to explode in unison, often in a climax lasting as little as a day. Two or three bouquets of a single species may occur in a season. The colors are never static. In January, it's the turn of pink *poui* (savannah oak) and yellow *poui* (black bark tree). By February, canary-bright *corteza amarillo* (*Tabebuia ochracea*) and the trumpet-shaped yellow blossoms of *Tabebuia chrysantha* dot the landscape. In March delicate pink *curao* appears. As the *curao* wanes, *Tabebuia rosea* bursts forth in subtle pinks, whites, and lilacs. The *malinche*—royal poinciana or flame tree—closes out the six-month parade of blossoming trees with a dramatic display as bright as red lipstick.

The Southern Plains

The Pan-American Highway (Hwy. 1) descends from the Central Highlands to the Pacific plains via Esparza, at the foot of the mountains about 15 kilometers (9.5 miles) east of Puntarenas, Costa Rica's main port on the Pacific.

PUNTARENAS

Five kilometers (3 miles) long but only five blocks wide at its widest, this sultry port town, 120 kilometers (75 miles) west of San José, is built on a long narrow spit—Puntarenas means "Sandy Point"—running west from the suburb of Cocal and backed to the north by a mangrove estuary; to the south are the Golfo de Nicoya and a beach cluttered with driftwood. Puntarenas has long been favored by Josefinos seeking R&R. The old wharves on the estuary side feature decrepit fishing boats leaning against ramshackle piers popular with pelicans.

The peninsula was colonized by the

Catedral de Puntarenas

Spaniards as early as 1522. The early port grew to prominence and was declared a free port in 1847, a year after completion of an ox-cart road from the Meseta Central. Oxcarts laden with coffee made the lumbering descent to Puntarenas in convoys; the beans were shipped from here via Cape Horn to Europe. It remained the country's main port until the Atlantic Railroad to Limón, on the Caribbean coast, was completed in 1890 (the railroad between San José and Puntarenas would not be completed for another 20 years). Earlier this century, Puntarenas also developed a large conch-pearl fleet. Some 80 percent of Porteños, as the inhabitants of Puntarenas are called, still make their living from the sea.

The town's main usefulness is as the departure point for day cruises to islands in the Golfo de Nicoya and for the ferries to Playa Naranjo and Paquera, on the Nicoya Peninsula. Cruise ships berth at the terminal opposite Calle Central.

Sights

The tiny **Catedral de Puntarenas** (Ave. Central, Calles 5/7), built in 1902, abuts the renovated **Antigua Comandancia de la Plaza,** a fortress-style building complete with tiny battlements and bars on its windows. It

once served as a barracks and a city jail. Today it houses the refurbished **Museo Histórico Marino** (tel. 506/2661-0387, 9:45am-noon and 1pm-5:15pm Tues.-Sun., free), a history museum that has exhibits on city life from the pre-Columbian and coffee eras. Adjacent is the **Casa de la Cultura** (tel. 506/2661-1394, 10am-4pm Mon.-Fri., free), with an art gallery that doubles as a venue for literary, musical, and artistic events.

Everything of importance seems to happen along the **Paseo de los Turistas,** a boulevard paralleling the Golfo de Nicoya and abuzz with vendors, beachcombers, and locals flirting and trying to keep cool in the water. The boulevard's beachfront park is studded with contemporary statues.

On the north side of the peninsula, the sheltered gulf shore—the estuary—is lined with fishing vessels in various states of decrepitude. Roseate spoonbills, storks, and other birds pick among the shallows.

Entertainment and Events

Every mid-July the city honors Carmen, Virgin of the Sea, in the annual **Festival Perla del Pacífico** (Sea Festival), a boating regatta with boats decorated in colorful flags and banners. The local Chinese community

cannon outside the Museo Histórico Marino, Puntarenas

Puntarenas

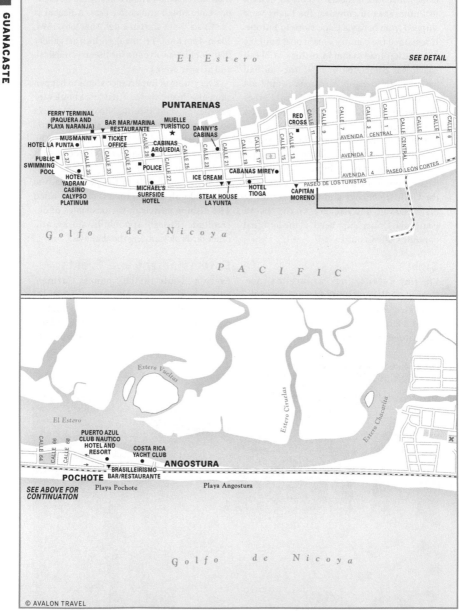

SEE DETAIL

El Estero

PUNTARENAS

FERRY TERMINAL
(PAQUERA AND
PLAYA NARANJA)

HOTEL LA PUNTA ●

PUBLIC
SWIMMING
POOL

HOTEL
YADRAN/
CASINO
CALYPSO
PLATINUM

MUSMANNI ▼
■ TICKET
OFFICE

BAR MAR/MARINA
RESTAURANTE

CABINAS
ARGUEDIA

POLICE

MICHAEL'S
SURFSIDE
HOTEL

C 37

CALLE 35

CALLE 33

CALLE 31

CALLE 29

CALLE 27

CALLE 25

CALLE 23

MUELLE
TURÍSTICO
★

DANNY'S
CABINAS

ICE CREAM

STEAK HOUSE
LA YUNTA

CALLE 21

CABAÑAS MIREY ●

CALLE 19

HOTEL
TIOGA

CALLE 17

CALLE 15

CALLE 13

CALLE 11

RED
CROSS

CALLE 9

CAPITÁN
MORENO

PASEO DE LOS TURISTAS

CALLE 7

AVENIDA CENTRAL

AVENIDA 2

AVENIDA 4

CALLE 3

CALLE 1

CALLE CENTRAL

CALLE 2

CALLE 4

CALLE 6

PASEO LEÓN CORTES

Golfo de Nicoya

PACIFIC

Estero Vueltas

El Estero

Estero Ciruelas

Estero Chacarita

CALLE 64

CALLE 66

CALLE 68

PUERTO AZUL
CLUB NÁUTICO
HOTEL AND
RESORT

COSTA RICA
YACHT CLUB

▼ BRASILLEIRISMO
BAR/RESTAURANTE

POCHOTE

ANGOSTURA

SEE ABOVE FOR
CONTINUATION

Playa Pochote

Playa Angostura

Golfo de Nicoya

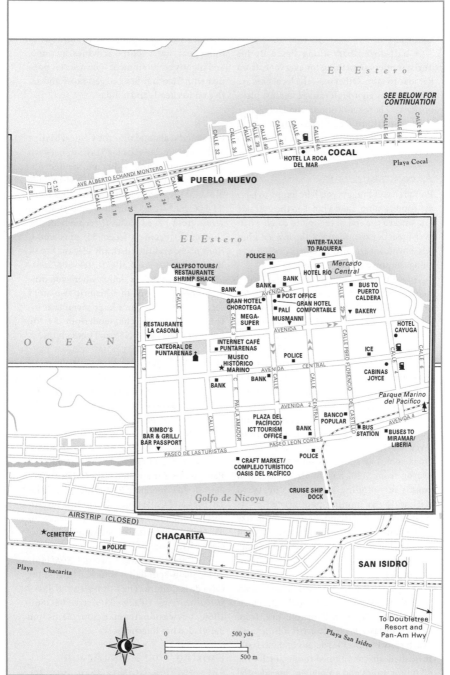

El Estero

SEE BELOW FOR
CONTINUATION

CALLE 42
CALLE 44
CALLE 46
CALLE 54
CALLE 56
CALLE 58
CALLE 32
CALLE 34
CALLE 36
CALLE 38
CALLE 40

COCAL
HOTEL LA ROCA
DEL MAR
Playa Cocal

AVE ALBERTO ECHANDI MONTERO
PUEBLO NUEVO
C 12
C 10
C 8
CALLE 16
CALLE 18
CALLE 20
CALLE 22
CALLE 24
CALLE 26

O C E A N

El Estero

WATER-TAXIS
TO PAQUERA

POLICE HQ

CALYPSO TOURS/
RESTAURANTE
SHRIMP SHACK

Mercado
HOTEL RÍO Central

BANK
BANK
BANK
BANK

AVENIDA 3

BUS TO
PUERTO
CALDERA

POST OFFICE
GRAN HOTEL
CHOROTEGA
PALÍ
MEGA-
SUPER
MUSMANNI

GRAN HOTEL
COMFORTABLE

BAKERY

CALLE 7
CALLE 3

RESTAURANTE
LA CASONA

CALLE 2

HOTEL
CAYUGA

AVENIDA 1

CATEDRAL DE
PUNTARENAS

INTERNET CAFÉ
PUNTARENAS

POLICE

CALLE PBRO FLORENCIO

ICE

CALLE 8

MUSEO
HISTÓRICO
MARINO

CALLE 6

AVENIDA CENTRAL

CALLE 9

CABINAS
JOYCE

BANK

C E

CALLE 4

BANK

AVENIDA 2

PASEO LEÓN CORTES

Parque Marino
del Pacífico

CALLE 5

CALLE CENTRAL

DEL CASTILLO

AVENIDA 4

PLAZA DEL
PACÍFICO/
ICT TOURISM
OFFICE

BANCO
POPULAR

BANK

KIMBO'S
BAR & GRILL/
BAR PASSPORT

PASEO DE LAS TURISTAS

PASEO LEÓN CORTES

BUS
STATION

BUSES TO
MIRAMAR/
LIBERIA

POLICE

PASEO AMADOR

CRAFT MARKET/
COMPLEJO TURÍSTICO
OASIS DEL PACÍFICO

CRUISE SHIP
DOCK

Golfo de Nicoya

AIRSTRIP (CLOSED)

CEMETERY

CHACARITA

POLICE

SAN ISIDRO

Playa Chacarita

To Doubletree
Resort and
Pan-Am Hwy

0   500 yds

0   500 m

Playa San Isidro

contributes dragon boats. In summer, concerts and plays are put on at the Casa de la Cultura.

A half-dozen bars along Paseo de los Turistas offers something for everyone, from karaoke to salsa. Otherwise, the local bars are overwhelmingly rough (guard against pickpockets). There's a casino in the Doubletree Resort by Hilton Puntarenas, and **Casino Calypso Platinum** is at the Hotel Yadran (Paseo de las Turistas, Calle 35).

Accommodations

Puntarenas is muggy; you'll be happy to have air-conditioning. Take a hotel on the gulf side and toward the end of the spit to catch whatever breezes exist. Many of the low-end hotels downtown are volatile refuges of ill repute; things improve west of downtown.

Now in French Canadian hands, **Hotel La Punta** (Ave. 1, Calles 35/37, tel. 506/2661-0696, www.hotellapunta.net, low season $60 s/d, high season $70 s/d) is a good choice if you want to catch the early-morning ferry to Nicoya; it's just one block away. The 12 air-conditioned rooms are pleasant enough and have spacious hot-water baths. Upper rooms have balconies. It has a small pool and a restaurant, plus parking.

The venerable, comfortable, yet undistinguished **Hotel Tioga** (Paseo de los Turistas, Aves. 15/17, tel. 506/2661-0271, www.hoteltioga.com, low season from $88 s/d, high season from $110) has 46 air-conditioned rooms surrounding a compact courtyard with a tiny swimming pool graced by its own palm-shaded island. Rooms vary in size and quality; all have TVs and phones but not all have hot water. There's secure parking. Rates include breakfast in the fourth-floor restaurant.

Perfect for families, **Doubletree Resort by Hilton Central Pacific** (tel. 506/2663-0808, http://doubletree1.hilton.com, from $218 all-inclusive) is an attractive all-inclusive beach resort with 230 spacious and modestly furnished air-conditioned rooms, including 87 junior suites and an opulent presidential suite, all with contemporary furnishings, including 27-inch flat-screen TVs. Heaps of facilities include an immense free-form swimming pool, water sports, activities, a casino, and nightly entertainment. The resort is popular with Tico families and gets noisy and active on weekends and holidays.

Food

Cheap *sodas* abound near the Central Market and along the Paseo de los Turistas, between Calles Central and 3. Recommended options along Paseo de los Turistas include **Matobe's** (Paseo de los Turistas, Calles 15/17, tel. 506/2661-3498, 11am-10pm daily), which serves fresh-baked pastas (I recommend the chicken fettuccine alfredo, $5) plus wood-fired pizza; and the rustically elegant **Steak House La Yunta** (Calle 21, tel. 506/2661-3216, 10am-midnight daily), where you dine on an open veranda of a historic two-story seafront house. It has a huge menu that includes shrimp, ceviche, tenderloin ($9-10), tongue in beet sauce ($8), and pork chops.

Information and Services

The city's **visitor information office** (tel. 506/2661-0337, ictpuntarenas@ict.go.cr, 8am-5pm Mon.-Fri.) is above Bancrédito, opposite the cruise-ship pier.

The **Monseñor Sanabria Hospital** (tel. 506/2630-8000) is eight kilometers (5 miles) east of town. There's a branch hospital at Paseo de los Turistas and Calle 9. The **police station** (tel. 506/2661-0740) is at Paseo de los Turistas and Calle Central; criminal investigation is handled by the **OIJ** (tel. 506/2630-0377). The **post office** is on Avenida 3, Calles Central/1.

Puntarenas Cyber Café (tel. 506/2661-4024, 10am-8pm daily) is tucked behind the Casa de la Cultura. The **Coonatramar ferry terminal** (Ave. 3, Calles 33/35, tel. 506/2661-1069, www.coonatramar.com, 8am-5pm daily) also has Internet service.

Getting There and Around

Empresarios Unidos (San José tel.

506/2222-8231, Puntarenas tel. 506/2661-3138) buses depart San José ($3) from Calle 16, Avenidas 10/12, every hour 6am-7pm daily. Buses also depart for Puntarenas from Monteverde (tel. 506/2645-5159) at 4:30am, 6am, and 3pm daily, and from Liberia (tel. 506/2663-1752) eight times 5am-3:30pm daily. Return buses depart the Puntarenas bus station (Calle 2, Paseo de los Turistas) for San José 4am-7pm daily; for Monteverde at 7:50am, 1:50pm, and 2:15pm daily; and Liberia 4:50am-8:30pm daily. Interbus (tel. 506/4100-0888, www.interbusonline. com) operates minibus shuttles from San José ($30) and popular tourist destinations in Nicoya and Guanacaste.

Buses ply Avenidas Central and 2. Coopepuntarenas (tel. 506/2663-1635) offers taxi service.

Car-and-passenger ferries for the Nicoya Peninsula leave the Coonatramar ferry terminal (Ave. 3, Calles 33/35, tel. 506/2661-9011, www.coonatramar.com, 8am-5pm daily). Buses marked "Ferry" operate along Avenida Central to the terminal ($2).

The Costa Rica Yacht Club and Marina (tel. 506/2661-0784, www.costaricayachtclub. com) has facilities for yachters.

COSTA DE PÁJAROS

At San Gerardo, on the Pan-American Highway, 40 kilometers (25 miles) north of Puntarenas, a paved road leads west to Punta Morales and the Golfo de Nicoya. There's fabulous bird-watching among the mangroves that line the shore—known as the Costa de Pájaros—stretching north to Manzanillo, the estuary of the Río Abangaritos, and beyond to the estuary of the Río Tempisque. The mangroves are home to ibis, herons, pelicans, parrots, egrets, and caimans. You can follow this coast road through cattle country to Highway 18, five kilometers (3 miles) east of the Tempisque bridge.

Refugio Nacional de Vida Silvestre La Enseñada (La Enseñada National Wildlife Refuge) is near Abangaritos, two kilometers (1.2 miles) north of Manzanillo, 17 kilometers (11 miles) from the Pan-American Highway. The 380-hectare (939-acre) wildlife refuge is part of a family-run cattle finca and salt farm, with nature trails and a lake replete with waterfowl and crocodiles.

The Reserva Biológica Isla Pájaros (Birds Island Biological Reserve) is about 600 meters (0.4 miles) offshore from Punta Morales. The 3.8-hectare (9.4-acre) reserve protects a colony of brown pelicans and other

cruise ship in Puntarenas

seabirds. Access is restricted to biological researchers.

A must-visit is **Santuario de Lapas el Manantial** (El Manantial Macaw Sanctuary, tel. 506/2661-5419 or 506/8823-2460, www. santuariolapas.com, 7am-5pm daily), a macaw-breeding center about six kilometers (4 miles) west of the Pan-American Highway at Aranjuez. Both scarlet and green macaws are raised here and fly free and unrestricted. There are also monkeys, tapirs, sloths, and other animals confiscated by the government from the illegal pet trade. Call ahead, as the entrance gate is usually locked.

Getting There
Buses depart Puntarenas for the Costa de Pájaros from Avenida Central, Calle 4.

LAS JUNTAS DE ABANGARES
Small it may be, but Las Juntas—at the base of the Cordillera Tilarán about 50 kilometers (31 miles) north of Esparza and six kilometers (4 miles) east of Highway 1 (the turnoff is at Km. 164, about 12 kilometers/7.5 miles north of the Río Lagarto and the turnoff for Monteverde)—figures big in the region's history. When gold was discovered in the nearby mountains in 1884, it sparked a gold rush. Hungry prospectors came from all over the world to sift the earth for nuggets, making Las Juntas a Wild West town. Inflated gold prices have lured many *oreros* (miners) back to the old mines and streams, and about 40 kilograms (88 pounds) of gold are recovered each week.

The *María Cristina,* a pint-size locomotive that sits in the town plaza, once hauled ore for the Abangares Gold Fields Company and dates from 1904. The *oreros* are honored with a **statue** in a triangular plaza on the northeast corner of town, which is splashed with colorful flowers and trim pastel-painted houses. A tree-lined main boulevard and streets paved with interlocking stones add to the orderliness.

If you're intrigued by this history, check out the **Ecomuseo Las Minas** (tel. 506/2662-0033, www.puebloantiguo.com, 8am-5pm Tues.-Fri., $5), displaying mining equipment at the entrance of an old mine. It is usually closed; call ahead to Centro Turístico Pueblo Antiguo (tel. 506/2662-0033), to which it belongs. It's near the hamlet of La Sierra, three kilometers (2 miles) east of Las Juntas. The center offers a Gold Mine Adventure down dank candlelit tunnels (helmets and flashlights provided, $20). **Mina Tours** (tel. 506/2662-0753, www.minatours.com) in Las Juntas also offers tours of a miners' cooperative; or book direct through the **Asociación Nacional de Mineros** (tel. 506/2662-0846), which has an office 500 meters (0.3 miles) east of town.

The road northeast from the triangular plaza leads into the Cordillera Tilarán via Candelaria and then (to the right) Monteverde or (to the left) Tilarán; a 4WD vehicle is recommended. In places the views are fantastic.

Getting There
Transportes Las Juntas (tel. 506/2258-5792 or 506/2695-5611) buses depart San José from Calle 14, Avenidas 1/3, at 10:45am and 5:30pm daily. Return buses to San José depart Las Juntas at 6:30am and 11:45pm daily. **Transportes Caribeños** (tel. 506/2669-1111) has a bus from Liberia at 4pm daily, returning at 5:30am daily.

Monteverde and Santa Elena

Monteverde, 35 kilometers (22 miles) north from the Pan-American Highway, means "Green Mountain," an appropriate name for one of the most idyllic pastoral settings in Costa Rica. Cows munch contentedly, and horse-drawn wagons loaded with milk cans still make the rounds in this world-famous community atop a secluded 1,400-meter-high (4,600-foot-high) plateau in the Cordillera de Tilarán. Monteverde is actually a sprawling agricultural community; the Reserva Biológica Bosque Nuboso Monteverde (Monteverde Cloud Forest Biological Reserve), which is what most visitors come to see, is a few kilometers southeast and higher up. A growing number of attractions are found north of Santa Elena, the main village, which has its own cloud-forest reserve. The two reserves are at different elevations and have different fauna and flora.

The reserves are within the Zona Protectora Arenal-Monteverde (Arenal-Monteverde Protected Zone). Created in 1991, it encompasses more than 30,000 hectares (74,000 acres) extending down both the Caribbean and Pacific slopes of the Cordillera de Tilarán, passing through eight distinct ecological zones, most notably cloud forest at higher elevations. Wind-battered elfin woods on exposed ridges are spectacularly dwarfed, whereas more protected areas have majestically tall trees festooned with orchids, bromeliads, ferns, and vines. Clouds sift through the forest primeval. February through May, quetzals are in the cloud forest. Later, they migrate downhill, where they can be seen around the hotels of Monteverde. Just after dawn is a good time to spot quetzals, which are particularly active in the early morning, especially in April and May.

The fame of the preserve has spawned an ever-increasing influx of tourists and a blossoming of attractions—the area is in danger of becoming overdeveloped and overpriced. The government's announcement, in 2013, that it would finally pave the road up to Monteverde will probably speed up the process.

ORIENTATION
The village of Santa Elena is the service center, with banks, stores, and bars. Populated by Tico families, Santa Elena is commonly considered to be Monteverde, although Monteverde proper is strung out along the road that leads up to the Reserva Biológica Bosque Nuboso Monteverde and is predominantly populated by the descendants of North American Quakers. Separating the two communities is the region of Cerro Plano.

★ MONTEVERDE CLOUD FOREST
The 14,200-hectare (35,090-acre) Reserva Biológica Bosque Nuboso Monteverde (Monteverde Cloud Forest Biological Reserve, tel. 506/2645-5122, www.reservamonteverde.com, 7am-4pm daily, adults $18, children and students $9), six kilometers (4 miles) east of Santa Elena, is owned and administered by the Tropical Science Center of Costa Rica. It protects more than 100 species of mammals, more than 400 species of birds, and more than 1,200 species of amphibians and reptiles. It is one of the few remaining habitats of all six indigenous species of the cat family: jaguar (on the lower slopes), ocelot, puma, margay, oncilla, and jaguarundi. Bird species include black guan, emerald toucanet, the critically endangered three-wattled bellbird, whose metallic "bonk!" call carries for almost three kilometers (2 miles), and 30 local hummingbird species. Hundreds of visitors arrive in hopes of seeing a resplendent quetzal; approximately 200 pairs nest in the reserve. Cognoscenti know that, ironically, the parking lot is perhaps the best place to see quetzals; in March 2014 it's where I saw a quetzal, perched like a

Monteverde and Santa Elena

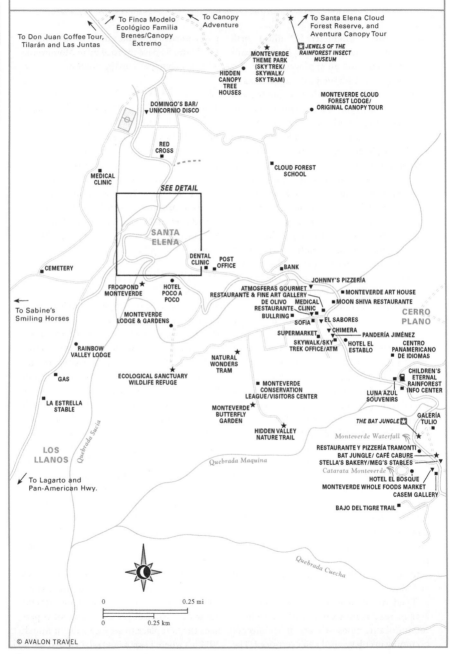

To Don Juan Coffee Tour, Tilarán and Las Juntas

To Finca Modelo Ecológico Familia Brenes/Canopy Extremo

To Canopy Adventure

To Santa Elena Cloud Forest Reserve, and Aventura Canopy Tour

JEWELS OF THE RAINFOREST INSECT MUSEUM

MONTEVERDE THEME PARK (SKY TREK/ SKYWALK/ SKY TRAM)

HIDDEN CANOPY TREE HOUSES

MONTEVERDE CLOUD FOREST LODGE/ ORIGINAL CANOPY TOUR

DOMINGO'S BAR/ UNICORNIO DISCO

RED CROSS

CLOUD FOREST SCHOOL

MEDICAL CLINIC

SEE DETAIL

SANTA ELENA

CEMETERY

DENTAL CLINIC

POST OFFICE

BANK

JOHNNY'S PIZZERÍA

To Sabine's Smiling Horses

FROGPOND MONTEVERDE

HOTEL POCO A POCO

ATMOSFERAS GOURMET RESTAURANTE & FINE ART GALLERY

MONTEVERDE ART HOUSE

MOON SHIVA RESTAURANTE

RESTAURANTE DE OLIVO

MEDICAL CLINIC

CERRO PLANO

MONTEVERDE LODGE & GARDENS

RESTAURANTE BULLRING

SOFIA

EL SABORES

RAINBOW VALLEY LODGE

SUPERMARKET

CHIMERA

PANDERÍA JIMÉNEZ

SKYWALK/SKY TREK OFFICE/ATM

HOTEL EL ESTABLO

CENTRO PANAMERICANO DE IDIOMAS

GAS

ECOLOGICAL SANCTUARY WILDLIFE REFUGE

NATURAL WONDERS TRAM

CHILDREN'S ETERNAL RAINFOREST INFO CENTER

MONTEVERDE CONSERVATION LEAGUE/VISITORS CENTER

LUNA AZUL SOUVENIRS

LA ESTRELLA STABLE

MONTEVERDE BUTTERFLY GARDEN

GALERÍA TULIO

THE BAT JUNGLE

HIDDEN VALLEY NATURE TRAIL

Monteverde Waterfall

LOS LLANOS

Quebrada Sucia

Quebrada Maquina

RESTAURANTE Y PIZZERÍA TRAMONTI
BAT JUNGLE/ CAFÉ CABURE
STELLA'S BAKERY/MEG'S STABLES

Catarata Monteverde

HOTEL EL BOSQUE
MONTEVERDE WHOLE FOODS MARKET
CASEM GALLERY

To Lagarto and Pan-American Hwy.

BAJO DEL TIGRE TRAIL

Quebrada Cuecha

0   0.25 mi

0   0.25 km

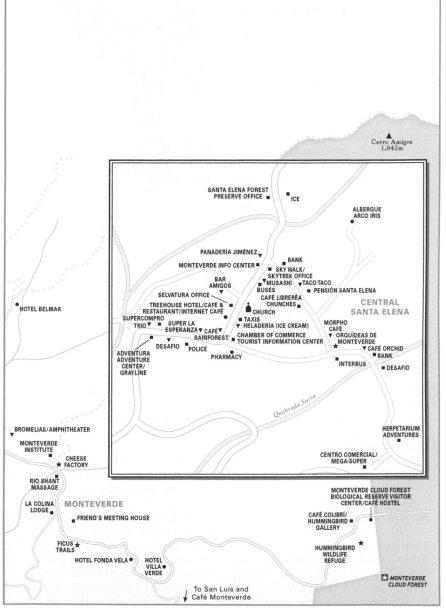

Cerro Amigos
1,842m

SANTA ELENA FOREST
PRESERVE OFFICE ■   ■ ICE

ALBERGUE
ARCO IRIS

PANADERÍA JIMÉNEZ ▼
MONTEVERDE INFO CENTER ■   ■ BANK
■ SKY WALK/
BAR   SKYTREK OFFICE
AMIGOS   ▼MUSASHI ▼TACO TACO
SELVATURA OFFICE ■   BUSES ■ ● PENSIÓN SANTA ELENA
▼   CAFÉ LIBRERÊA
TREEHOUSE HOTEL/CAFÉ &   CHUNCHES ■
RESTAURANT/INTERNET CAFÉ   ✝ CHURCH   **CENTRAL**
SUPERCOMPRO   ●   **SANTA ELENA**
TRIO▼   ■ TAXIS
SUPER LA   ▼ HELADERÍA (ICE CREAM)   MORPHO
ESPERANZA▼ CAFÉ▼   CAFÉ
▼   RAINFOREST ■ CHAMBER OF COMMERCE   ▼ ORQUÍDEAS DE
DESAFIO ■   TOURIST INFORMATION CENTER   ★ MONTEVERDE
● HOTEL BELMAR   ■ POLICE   ▼ CAFÉ ORCHID
ADVENTURA   ■ BANK
ADVENTURE   ■ PHARMACY   ■
CENTER/   INTERBUS   ■ DESAFIO
GRAYLINE

Quebrada Sucia

HERPETARIUM
ADVENTURES
■

▼ BROMELIAS/AMPHITHEATER
MONTEVERDE
INSTITUTE
■   CENTRO COMERCIAL/
★ CHEESE   MEGA-SUPER
FACTORY   ■

● RIO SHANT
MASSAGE   MONTEVERDE CLOUD FOREST
BIOLOGICAL RESERVE VISITOR
LA COLINA   CENTER/CAFÉ HOSTEL
LODGE ●   **MONTEVERDE**
■ FRIEND'S MEETING HOUSE   CAFÉ COLIBRÍ/
HUMMINGBIRD ■   ■
GALLERY

FICUS ★
TRAILS   HUMMINGBIRD ★
HOTEL FONDA VELA ●   HOTEL   WILDLIFE
VILLA   REFUGE
VERDE ●

To San Luis and   ✦ MONTEVERDE
Café Monteverde   CLOUD FOREST

museum piece, almost within reach. Go early in the morning.

The reserve has 13 kilometers (8 miles) of trails for day visitors concentrated in an area called The Triangle. Parts ooze with mud; other sections have been covered with raised wooden walkways. A maximum of 180 people are allowed on the trails at any one time. Access is first come, first served, except for those already booked on guided tours.

Longer trails requiring an overnight stay lead down the Pacific slopes. **Sendero Valle** leads to La Cascada, a triple waterfall, and continues via the valley of the Río Peñas Blancas to Pocosol, about 20 kilometers (12 miles) south of La Fortuna. These are for experienced Indiana Jones-type hikers only (the three basic backpacking shelters are closed until further notice). Reservations are essential, and a guide is obligatory for these longer trails.

If you want to hike alone, buy your ticket the day before and set out before the crowds. You increase your chances of seeing wildlife if you hike with a guide; reservations are advisable (book online at www.reservamonteverde. com, from $18). Three-hour guided tours (*caminatas*) are offered at 7:30am, noon, and 1:30pm daily (minimum 3 people, maximum 9 people, adults $32, students $18, including admission); hourly tours are planned. A five-hour bird-watching tour ($64 pp, including admission) is offered at 6am daily. A two-hour night hike ($17, with hotel transfers $22) is offered at 6:15pm daily.

Bring warm clothing and rain gear. You can rent rubber boots in many hotels. The visitors center rents binoculars ($10 per day, plus deposit) and sells a self-guided pamphlet, a trail map, and wildlife guides.

A café at the visitors center serves omelets ($1.75), burgers, sandwiches, mochas ($1), and other fare. A bus (tel. 506/2645-6296) departs Santa Elena for the reserve ($1 each way) at 6:15am, 7:20am, 9:20am, 1:20pm, and 3pm daily, returning at 6:45am, 7:45am, 11:30am, 2pm, and 4pm daily. Most hotels can arrange transportation. A taxi from Santa Elena

resplendent quetzal

should cost about $10 one-way, but there are reports of gouging. Parking is available.

SANTA ELENA CLOUD FOREST

The 310-hectare (766-acre) **Reserva Bosque Nuboso Santa Elena** (Santa Elena Cloud Forest Reserve, tel. 506/2645-5390, www. reservasantaelena.org, 7am-4pm daily, adults $15, students and children $7) is five kilometers (3 miles) northeast of Santa Elena, and a 4WD vehicle is required to gain access. Owned by the Santa Elena community, it boasts all the species claimed by its eastern neighbor—plus spider monkeys, which are absent from the Monteverde reserve. It has four one-way trails that range 1.4 to 4.8 kilometers (0.9-3 miles) and an observation tower with views toward Volcán Arenal. At a higher elevation than Monteverde reserve, it tends to be cloudier and wetter.

Guides are available, as are dormitory accommodations. Guided three-hour hikes ($17) are offered at 7am, 9am, 11am, and 1pm

hikers in Monteverde Cloud Forest

Elena at 6:45am, 11am, and 2:30pm daily. A shared taxi ($2 pp) leaves Santa Elena village at 6:45am, 8am, 10:30am, 12:30pm, and 2pm daily, but you must book the day before. A regular taxi costs about $10 each way.

BOSQUE ETERNO DE LOS NIÑOS

Surrounding the Reserva Biológica Bosque Nuboso Monteverde on three sides, the **Bosque Eterno de Los Niños** (Children's Eternal Rainforest) is the largest private reserve in Central America. It is administered by the **Monteverde Conservation League** (tel. 506/2645-5003, www.friendsoftherainforest.org). The dream of a rainforest saved by children began in 1987 at a small primary school in rural Sweden. A study of tropical forests prompted nine-year-old Roland Teinsuu to ask what he could do to keep the rainforest and the animals that live in it safe from destruction. Young Roland's question launched a group campaign to raise money to help the league buy and save threatened rainforest in Costa Rica. Roland and his classmates raised enough money to buy six hectares (15 acres) of rainforest at a cost of $250 per hectare. Out of this initial success, a group of children dedicated to saving the tropical rainforest formed Barnens Regnskog (Children's Rainforest). The vision took hold, sweeping the globe, with contributions flocking in from the far corners. The original preserve, established

daily; there is also a 90-minute night tour at 7pm daily. You can buy trail maps and a self-guided trail booklet—and rent rubber boots ($1)—at the visitors center.

The reserve is the site of the **Monteverde Cloud Forest Ecological Center,** a farm that educates youngsters and local farmers on forest ecology and conservation.

Shuttles for ticket-holders leave Santa

The Disappearance of the Golden Toad

The Reserva Biológica Bosque Nuboso Monteverde owes its existence in part to a brilliant neon-orange arboreal toad—*sapo dorado* (*Bufo periglenes*)—discovered in 1964 and so stunning that one biologist harbored "a suspicion that someone had dipped the examples in enamel paint." The males are the orange ones; females, which are larger, are yellow and black with patches of scarlet. Monteverde is the only known home of this fabulous creature. But don't expect to see one; it is already extinct. Although in 1986 it could be seen in large quantities, by 1988 very few remained. No sightings have been made since 1996. These creatures may now exist only on the cover of tourism brochures, victims of a deadly fungus that has devastated the world's frog populations in recent decades.

near Monteverde in 1988, has grown to more than 22,000 hectares (54,000 acres).

It is accessed via the **Bajo del Tigre** (tel. 506/2645-5923, 7:30am-5:30pm daily, adults $20, children $12), off the main road, just above the CASEM Gallery. This section of the reserve is at a lower elevation than the Reserva Biológica Bosque Nuboso Monteverde and thus offers a different variety of plant and animal life. Quetzals are more easily seen here, for example, than higher up in the wetter, mistier cloud forest. Facilities include a Children's Nature Center, a self-guided interpretative trail, an arboretum, a visitors center, and a library. Guided two-hour tours ($20, with transfers $22) are offered at 5:30am (for bird-watchers), 8am, 2pm, and 5:30pm (a night tour) daily.

There are also two field stations: at Poco Sol, on the lower eastern slopes, with eight rooms (six with private baths) for 26 people as well as 10 kilometers (6 miles) of hiking trails; and San Gerardo, at 1,220 meters (4,000 feet) elevation, a 3.5-kilometer (2-mile) walk from the Santa Elena reserve, with accommodations for 26 people and six kilometers (4 miles) of trails. Guides are available by request.

SAN LUIS BIOLOGICAL RESERVE

Reserva Biológica San Luis (tel. 506/2645-8049, www.cct.or.cr, day visits $10, students $6, guided tour $20, horseback rides $10 per hour) is affiliated with the Tropical Science Center of Costa Rica and doubles as an integrated tourism, research, and education project on a 70-hectare (173-acre) farm and botanical garden at San Luis, eight kilometers (5 miles) southeast of Monteverde. The turnoff is immediately east of Hotel Fonda Vela on the road to the Monteverde reserve; it's a steep descent. Resident biologists work with members of the San Luis community to develop a model for sustainable development.

The station offers a wide range of activities: horseback rides, bird-watching, cloud-forest hiking (plus a hike to the San Luis waterfall), night walks, and hands-on laboratory study.

Open-air classes are given, including an intensive seven-day tropical biology course. You can even help farm or participate in scientific research.

It has a cozy wood-paneled bunkhouse— a former milking shed—with 30 bunks and shared baths, and four rooms with 2 to 12 beds each. It also has a four-room, 16-bed bungalow with private baths and verandas, plus 12 *cabinas* for 3 to 4 people each. Tico fare is cooked over a woodstove and served family-style. Lodging costs $49 pp in the dorm, $79 s or $144 d in the bungalow, and $102 s, $192 d in the cabins, which includes all meals and activities.

A taxi from Monteverde costs about $15.

WILDLIFE EXHIBITS
★ Jewels of the Rainforest Insect Museum

The **Jewels of the Rainforest Insect Museum** (tel. 506/2645-5929, www.selvatura.com, 7am-5pm daily, $15), at Selvatura, three miles northeast of Santa Elena, displays more than 50,000 insects, yet it's just a small fraction of Richard Whitten's findings from more than 50 years of collecting. It's the largest private collection of big, bizarre, and beautiful butterflies, beetles, and other bugs in the world. And it's surely is the most colorful—a veritable kaleidoscope of shimmering greens, neon blues, startling reds, silvers, and golds. Whitten began collecting "bugs" at a tender age; today his 1,900 boxes include more than one million specimens, many of them collected in Costa Rica. Part of the exhibit is dedicated to a collection of every known species in the country. Some beetles are bigger than your fist; some moths outsize a salad plate. Other exhibits include shimmering beetles displayed against black velvet, like opal jewelry, and boxes of bugs majestically turned into caskets of gems.

Covering 232 square meters (2,500 square feet), exhibits include a Biodiversity Bank with dozens of spectacular and informative displays; a wall of Neotropical Butterflies; a World of Beetles, from Tutankhamen scarabs to the giants of the beetle word; a Phasmid Room (stick insects and their relatives); and a Silk Room, displaying elegant moths. The dynamic displays combine art, science, music, and video to entertain and educate about insect mimicry, protective coloration and other forms of camouflage, prey-predator relationships, and more. A 279-square-meter (3,000-square-foot) auditorium screens fascinating videos.

Selvatura also has a hummingbird garden ($5), a vast domed butterfly garden ($15), and a reptile exhibit ($15). Guided nature hikes ($45) are offered.

★ The Bat Jungle

The Bat Jungle (tel. 506/2645-7701, www. batjungle.com, 9am-7:30pm daily, adults $12, students and children $10), between the gas station and the cheese factory, is the first in Costa Rica to provide an insight into the life of bats (Monteverde has at least 65 species). Eight species of live bats flit, feed, and mate within a sealed enclosure behind a wall of glass. Fascinating exhibits illuminate bat ecology and an auditorium screens documentaries. The guided tour is truly fascinating and illuminating. Guaranteed, you won't leave here without a deep admiration for these adorable and much misunderstood creatures. You can even don giant ears to get a sense for bats' supersize sonar hearing.

Monteverde Theme Park

The impressive Frog Pond of Monteverde, by which the Monteverde Theme Park (tel. 506/2645-6320, 9:30am-8:30pm daily, adults $12, children and students $10), on the south side of Santa Elena, is better known, displays 28 species of frogs and amphibians, from the red-eyed tree frog and transparent frogs to the elephantine marine toad, all housed in large, well-arranged display cases. It also has salamanders and a few snakes, plus termites and other bugs to be fed to the frogs, as well as a *mariposario* (butterfly garden, adults $12, children $10, $20 with Frog Pond). Evening visits are best, when the frogs become active.

Admission cost is valid for two entries, so you can see both daytime and nocturnal species.

Herpetarium Adventures

The Herpetarium Adventures (tel. 506/2645-6002, www.skyadventures.travel, 9am-8pm daily, adults $12, students $10, children $6, including guide), previously called the Serpentario, on the eastern fringe of Santa Elena village, lets you get up close and personal with an array of coiled constrictors and venomous vipers as well as their prey: frogs, chameleons, and the like. The dreaded fer-de-lance is here, along with 30 or so other species staring at you from behind thick panes of glass.

Monteverde Butterfly Garden

The Monteverde Butterfly Garden (tel. 506/2645-5512, www.monteverdebutterfly-garden.com, 8:30am-4pm daily, adults $15, students $10, children $5, including 1-hour guided tour), signed off the main road about one mile east of Santa Elena, features a nature center and three distinct habitats: a 450-square-meter (4,800-square-foot) netted butterfly flyway and two greenhouses representing lowland forest and mid-elevation forest habitats. Together they are filled with native plant species and hundreds of tropical butterflies representing more than 40 species. Fascinating guided tours begin in the visitors center, where butterflies and other bugs are mounted on display and rhinoceros beetles, stick insects, and tarantulas crawl around inside display cases. There's a computer station with interactive software about butterflies, plus an auditorium where videos are shown. Go mid-morning, when the butterflies become active (and most visitors are in the reserve).

Orquídeas de Monteverde

Orquídeas de Monteverde (Monteverde Orchid Garden, tel. 506/2645-5308, www. monteverdeorchidgarden.net, 8am-5pm daily, adults $10, students $7), in the heart of Santa Elena, took five years of arduous work to collate the results of the Monteverde Orchid Investigation Project, an ongoing effort to document and research local orchids. Short paths wind through the compact garden, displaying almost 450 species native to the region arranged in 22 groups ("subtribes"), each marked with an educational placard. Miniatures are preponderant, including the world's smallest flower, *Platystele jungermannioides,* about the size of a pinhead (fortunately, you are handed a magnifying glass upon arrival).

Finca Ecológica

Finca Ecológica (Ecological Sanctuary Wildlife Refuge, tel. 506/2645-5869, www.santuarioecologico.com, 7am-6pm daily, adults $10, students and children $8), on the same road as the Butterfly Garden, has six signed trails through the 48-hectare (119-acre) property, which has waterfalls. You have an excellent chance of seeing coatimundis, sloths, agoutis, porcupines, white-faced monkeys, butterflies, and birds. It offers a twilight tour (adults $25, students $20, children $15, including transfers) at 5pm daily.

Santamaría Night Walk

The great majority of critters in the cloud forest are nocturnal. To see them, take a guided tour at **Finca Agroturística Santamaría** (tel. 506/2645-6548, www.nightwalksantamarias.com, $22 including transfers), a great chance to spot sloths, snakes, and all manner of insects in this 10-hectare (25-acre) reserve to the northeast of Santa Elena.

FARM AND FOOD TOURS

Coffee is grown on the slopes just below Santa Elena and Monteverde; some three dozen small-scale coffee producers make up the Santa Elena cooperative. The **Don Juan Coffee Tour** (tel. 506/2645-7100, www.donjuancoffeetour.com, adults $30, children $12), offered at 8am, 10am, 1pm, and 3pm daily, provides an insight into coffee production.

The **El Trapiche Tour** (tel. 506/2645-7780, www.eltrapichetour.com, 10am and 3pm Mon.-Sat., 3pm Sun., adults $32, students $28, children $12) offers a more rounded experience that teaches about production of a wide range of crops, from coffee to sugarcane; the tour includes a ride in an ox-drawn cart. At **Finca Modelo Ecológica** (tel. 506/2645-5581, www.familiabrenestours.com, 6am and 3pm daily, adults $15, students and children $12) the Brenes family offers a tour of its

owner David Makynen at Monteverde Butterfly Garden

Costa Rica's Quaker Village

Monteverde was founded in 1951 by a group of 44 American Quakers—most from Fairhope, Alabama—who had refused to register for the draft as a matter of conscience. Led by John Campbell and Wilford "Wolf" Guindon, they chose Costa Rica for a new home because it had done away with its army. They built roads and cleared much of the virgin forest for dairy farming. They decided to make cheese because it was the only product that could be stored and moved to market without spoiling along a muddy oxcart trail. Cheese is still a mainstay of the local economy, and the Quaker organization is still active in Monteverde. It meets every Wednesday morning at the Friends Meeting House; visitors are welcome.

Don't expect to find the Quakers walking down the road dressed like the guy on the oatmeal box. *Cuaquerismo* (Quakerism) in Monteverde is a low-key affair.

organic dairy farm two kilometers (1.2 miles) north of Santa Elena.

La Lechería (Cheese Factory, tel. 506/2645-5436, 7:30am-5pm Mon.-Sat., 7:30am-4pm Sun.), in Monteverde, is famous for its quality cheeses. Production began in 1953 when the original Quaker settlers bought 50 Jersey cattle and began producing pasteurized Monteverde gouda cheese. The factory produces 14 types of cheese—from parmesan and emmentaler to Danish-style dambo and Monte Rico, the best-seller. Guided tours (tel. 506/2645-7090, www.monteverdecheesefactory.com, 9am and 2pm Mon.-Sat., adults $10, students and children $8) are offered.

ENTERTAINMENT AND EVENTS

Bromelias (tel. 506/2645-6272, 9am-5pm daily) hosts live music and occasional theater in the Monteverde Amphitheater, an open-air performance space. Bring a cushion to soften the iron-hard seating. In Santa Elena, Restaurante Don Juan (tel. 506/2661-7115) has live music upstairs (7pm Fri.-Sun.).

For a taste of local working-class color, wet your whistle at Bar Amigos (Monteverde, tel. 506/2645-5071, www.baramigos.com, noon-midnight daily), which has pool tables and karaoke; or at Unicornios (tel. 506/2645-6282, noon-midnight daily), a rough-and-tumble bar on the northwest side of Santa Elena. Both have pool tables. Unicornios has karaoke on Thursday. The

grooviest dance spot midweek is Taberna (tel. 506/2645-5883), on the east side of Santa Elena, with a nightly disco (free).

SPORTS AND RECREATION
Canopy Tours

An intriguing way to explore the Reserva Bosque Nuboso Santa Elena is by ascending into the forest canopy on a guided Sky Walk (tel. 506/2645-5238, www.skywalk.co.cr), which offers a monkey's-eye view of things. You walk along five suspension bridges and platforms and 1,000 meters (3,300 feet) of pathways that allow viewing from ground level to the treetops, where you are right in there with the epiphytes. Two-hour tours (adults $35, students $28, children $21) depart at 7:30am, 9:30am, 10:30am, 12:30pm, 1:30pm, and 3pm daily.

The same company offers a two-hour Sky Trek (adults $71, students $57, children $45) for the more adventurous. You'll whiz through the canopy in a harness attached to a zip line that runs between three treetop canopies, spanning two kilometers (1.2 miles). The tour starts with a ride on the Sky Tram cable car (which can only be taken in conjunction with the Sky Walk or Sky Trek).

Selvatura (tel. 506/2645-5929, www.selvatura.com, 7am-5pm daily), two kilometers (1.2 miles) north of Sky Walk, has a canopy exploration with three kilometers (2 miles) of suspended bridges ($30) and an 18-platform zip-line canopy tour (adults $45, students $40, children $30). Tours are at 8.30am, 11am, 1pm, and 2:30pm daily. The **Aventura Canopy Tour** (tel. 506/2645-6388, www.monteverdeadventure.com), off the road to the Sky Walk, has 16 zip-line cables (tours at 8am, 11am, 1pm, and 3pm daily, adults $45, children $35) plus suspended walkways (adults $35, children $25).

The canopy tour craze began at Monteverde Cloud Forest Lodge, where **The Original Canopy Tour** (tel. 506/2645-5243, www.canopytour.com, adults $45, students $35, children $25) was created. Zip-line tours are offered at 7:30am, 10:30am, and 2:30pm daily. A thrilling beginning is the forest hike and a clamber up the interior of a hollow strangler fig to reach the first platform.

Extremo Canopy (tel. 506/2645-6058, www.monteverdeextremo.com) has a 16-cable zip-line tour (8am, 11am, and 2pm daily, adults $40, students $30, children $25), plus bungee jumping ($60), a Tarzan swing ($35), canyoneering and a Superman line ($45), and horseback rides ($30).

Horseback Riding

The following have stables and rent horses (usually $10-15 per hour) and offer guided tours: **La Estrella Stables** (tel. 506/2645-5075); **Sabine's Smiling Horses** (tel. 506/2645-6894, www.horseback-riding-tour.com); and **Terra Viva** (tel. 506/2645-5454, www.terravivacr.com), which also offers tours of its organic dairy farm and cloud-forest reserve with trails. I recommend **Desafío Adventure Company** (tel. 506/2645-5874, www.desafiocostarica.com) for horseback trips to La Fortuna ($65); the four-hour horseback ride from Monteverde to Río Chiquito is followed by a one-hour boat ride across Laguna de Arenal, then a 30-minute Jeep ride to La Fortuna.

SHOPPING

The **Artisans' Cooperative of Santa Elena and Monteverde** (CASEM, tel. 506/2645-5190, www.monteverdeinfo.com/casem,

the Sky Tram at Monteverde

8am-5pm Mon.-Sat., 10am-4pm Sun.) features the handmade wares of 140 local artisans. Monteverde boasts numerous excellent galleries. **Artes Tulio** (tel. 506/2645-5567, www.artestulio.wix.com, 9am-6pm daily) sells the exquisite creations of gifted artist Marco Tulio Brenes. **Sarah's Gallery** (tel. 506/2645-7624, www.monteverdeartistsarahdowell.blogspot.com), also in Monteverde, offers lovely paintings of local flora and fauna by Sarah Dowell.

Bromelias (tel. 506/2645-6272, 10am-5:30pm Fri.-Wed., 10am-10pm Thurs.) sells books and quality batiks, jewelry, and carvings. The most impressive selection is at the **Art House** (tel. 506/2645-5275, www.monteverdearthouse.com), serving as both a workshop and gallery for everything from papier-mâché to pottery. The **Hummingbird Gallery** (tel. 506/2645-5030, 8:30am-4:30pm daily), 100 meters (330 feet) below the entrance to the Reserva Biológica Bosque Nuboso Monteverde, is well stocked with souvenirs.

In Santa Elena, **Librería Chunches** (tel./

fax 506/2645-5147, 8am-6:30pm Mon.-Fri.) sells English-language magazines and newspapers, plus natural history books and laminated *Costa Rican Field Guides.*

ACCOMMODATIONS

Accommodations may be difficult to obtain in dry season, when tour companies block space; book well ahead.

Under $25

You can camp at ★ **Pensión Santa Elena** (tel. 506/2645-5051, www.pensionsantaelena. com, camping $7 pp, dorm 8-9 pp, private room $16-84 s/d, cabin $35-70 s/d), which offers plenty of facilities, such as Wi-Fi and a café, in the heart of Santa Elena. Beloved of budget travelers, Pensión Santa Elena is owned by super-friendly Texan siblings Randa and Shannon, who earn high marks from readers. It has 25 basic rooms of varying sizes (some are dark). Some have private baths; all have hot water. A two-story annex has three rooms, a bar, and a restaurant, and you get secure parking. The hotel provides free use of a kitchen, plus laundry service ($2), Internet access, and travel information.

$25-50

At the southern entrance to Santa Elena, **Rainbow Valley Lodge** (tel. 506/2645-7015, www.rainbowvalleylodgecr.com, $30-50 s, $35-60 d), run by a pleasant Minnesotan, has two spacious, cross-lit, and cross-ventilated rooms in a lovely lodge with awesome views across the forested valley toward Monteverde. The lower of the two units has no valley views, but monkeys frolic in the treetops at fingertip distance. Readers rave about Rolf, the owner.

I love the dramatic Thai-style frontage of all-log **La Colina Lodge** (tel. 506/2645-5009, www.lacolinalodge.com, low season bunks from $10 pp, shared baths $25 s/d, private baths $45 s, $55 d), in Monteverde, which has three wood-paneled rooms with private baths, plus nine rooms with shared baths with hot water. The rooms boast handcrafted furnishings and Guatemalan bedspreads. Rooms with shared baths are small and dark. There's a TV room and a charming alpine restaurant.

$50-100

With easy access to Santa Elena, the splendid German-owned ★ **Albergue Arco Iris** (tel. 506/2645-5067, www.arcoirislodge.com, bunks from $27 s, $37 d, rooms from $67 s, $78 d) is run with Teutonic efficiency. It has six bunkrooms, 11 standard rooms, and two handsome stone-and-hardwood *cabinas* amid a spacious garden with deck chairs on a hillside backed by a two-hectare (5-acre) forest reserve. The *cabinas* feature terra-cotta tile floors and orthopedic mattresses with Guatemalan bedspreads. Best of all is the fabulous honeymoon suite with a kitchen, a sexy tiger-print bedspread in the upstairs bedroom, and gorgeous black-stone walls and sea-blue tiles in the bath with a two-person whirlpool tub. An airy restaurant offers breakfast only. Horses can be rented, and there's a library, laundry, and a safe.

Way up the hill close to the Monteverde reserve and exuding rusticity, **Hotel Villa Verde** (tel. 506/2645-4697, www.villaverdehotel.com, rooms $67 s, $90 d, villas $100 s, $120 d, including breakfast) has 16 cozy rooms with hardwood floors and five *cabinas* with roomy kitchenettes, a small lounge with a fireplace, and large bedrooms with four beds (one double, three singles). Villa suites have fireplaces and tubs, and voluminous tiled baths have hot water. The stone-and-timber lodge and its atrium restaurant offer a homey atmosphere and a game room. Horseback tours are offered.

$100-150

The nonsmoking **Monteverde Cloud Forest Lodge** (tel. 506/2645-5058, U.S. tel. 877-623-3198, www.cloudforestlodge.com, $90 s, $100 d), northeast of Santa Elena, earns raves from readers. It is surrounded by gardens set on a 25-hectare (62-acre) private forest reserve. The 18 wood-and-stone *cabinas* are clean and spacious, with large clerestory windows, peaked ceilings, and large baths. There's a large-screen TV and a VCR, plus free Wi-Fi. It has five kilometers (3 miles) of trails into forests, plus views of Nicoya from the deck. A daunting circular staircase leads to the entrance to the Sky Walk, at Santa Elena Cloud Forest Reserve.

The super-contemporary three-story **Hotel Poco a Poco** (tel. 506/2645-6000, www.hotelpocoapoco.com, low season from $99 s/d, high season from $134 s/d) is about 500 meters (0.3 miles) outside Santa Elena village center. Every year it seems to grow *poco a poco* (little by little), expanding from its original 5 rooms to 32 rooms with lively color schemes and sophisticated modern fittings, including cable TV, Wi-Fi, and DVD players (the hotel has a DVD library). It has an elegant restaurant, a spa, and a swimming pool—one of only two in Monteverde—that's heated and set in a flagstone sundeck with views.

Sufficiently alpine to make you want to yodel is the reclusive **Hotel Fonda Vela** (tel. 506/2645-5125, www.fondavela.com, rooms $105 s, $120 d, junior suites $140 s, $160 d), close to the Monteverde reserve. It has 20 standard rooms and 18 junior suites in nine buildings, all with rich hardwoods, picture windows, and recently upgraded furnishings that bring it stylishly into the 21st century. The suites are worth the splurge for their sitting rooms and large balconies. The landscaped grounds backed by forest are a delight for bird-watching.

Over $150

Earning high marks for its eco-consciousness and justifiably the latest addition to the Small Distinctive Hotels group, the family-run **Hotel Belmar** (tel. 506/2645-5201, www.hotelbelmar.net, low season $151-159 s/d, high season $189-199 s/d) is an ivy-clad Swiss-style grand dame with chalets that are the prettiest in Monteverde. Spacious rooms in the newer main building outshine the older cabins, not least for large baths with marble highlights; of its 28 comfortable rooms, four are family rooms. French doors in most rooms and lounges open onto balconies with views; a west-facing glass wall catches the sunset. The

lounge in the older building is a quiet spot for reading and for slide shows on Friday. The large restaurant has views. Hardy hikers can follow a trail to the mountain crest. Facilities include a whirlpool tub, a volleyball court, a pool table, and Internet access. Rates include tax.

The modern, eco-sensitive ★ **Monteverde Lodge & Gardens** (tel. 506/2645-5057, www.monteverdelodge.com, garden room $198 s/d, forest view $228 s/d year-round) is the best bargain in Monteverde, with spacious and elegant rooms that boast a classy chic that doesn't detract from the nature-lodge feel. Rooms feature large windows, two double beds with thick comforters and deluxe linens, plus phones, Wi-Fi, and well-lit solar-heated baths with stylish "salad bowl" sinks and large walk-in showers tiled with gray slate. Thoughtful touches include biscuits and coffee liqueurs by the bed at night. Opt for the upper Forest View rooms with balconies. A cavernous hotel entrance leads to an open-plan dining room and a cozy bar. The superb restaurant has a soaring beamed ceiling and wraparound windows overlooking beautifully landscaped grounds, where agoutis and other critters hang out. The bar has leather chairs, good for cuddling around an open hearth, and looks down on a large glass-enclosed whirlpool tub. The lodge is operated by Costa Rica Expeditions and is popular with bird-watching and nature groups. Rates include taxes.

Monteverde's largest, and some would argue most upscale, option is ★ **El Establo Hotel, Restaurant & Stable** (tel. 506/2645-5110, U.S. tel. 877-623-3198, www.hotelestablo.com, deluxe $216 s/d, suites $325 s/d year-round), which offers 155 standard rooms and junior suites, all with a stylish aesthetic. The original two-story wood-and-stone structure contains 20 standard rooms with cinderblock walls and wraparound windows; those on the ground floor open onto a wood-floored gallery lounge with deep-cushioned sofas and an open fireplace. Newer rooms are in a dramatic hillside annex (far enough that a shuttle ferries guests back and forth); all are junior suites with polished stone floors and exotic tile work, or upper-level carpeted suites with rattan furniture and king beds in lofts (plus double beds downstairs). You get rockers on your balcony, and there's a full-service spa, two restaurants, a swimming pool fit for a Balinese resort, and trails.

Monteverde hasn't been left out of the treehouse craze. Thus, ★ **Hidden Canopy B&B** (tel. 506/2645-5447, www.hiddencanopy.com, $225-445 s/d year-round) has four very private "tree-house chalets" accessed by lofty walkways. No ordinary tree houses, these chic and edgy all-wood units ooze class. The entire place is gorgeous, not least for its lush landscaped gardens. The ridge-top setting with vast views toward the Golfo de Nicoya is sublime. Two cabins are bi-level with two bedrooms. The others are single-story one-bedroom units; one is a honeymoon suite with a gas fire and a whirlpool tub. Owner Jennifer King also rents two rooms in the lodge, which has a fabulous lounge and a stone deck that's the setting for daily sunset teas. Furnishings include queen and king beds made of tree roots, with down comforters, and a hanging basket chair in which to soak up the forest views.

FOOD

I frequently dine at the **Morpho Café** (tel. 506/2645-7373, www.morphosrestaurant. com, 11am-9pm daily), in the heart of Santa Elena. It's known for its salads, sandwiches, great burgers, pastas, *casados* (set lunches, $4), and a house special of beef tenderloin with Monteverde blue cheese ($18). A copycat with a difference, the **Treehouse Café & Restaurant** (tel. 506/2645-5751, www.treehouse.cr, 11am-10pm daily), also in central Santa Elena, is built around a tree. Its menu ranges from burritos to fondues. My favorite? Chocolate fondue with brandy ($34 for 2 people).

The quaint, colorful **Dulce Marzo Bakery & Café** (tel. 506/2645-6568, 11am-7pm daily), in Cerro Plano, is good for wraps, sandwiches, and cookies. Chef Lisa Peters's peanut butter

cup specifically is to die for. For breakfast, try **Stella's Bakery** (tel. 506/2645-5560, 6am-6pm daily) in Monteverde. The rustic setting is perfect for enjoying granola with homemade yogurt ($2), pancakes, omelets, doughnuts, sandwiches, and great milk shakes ($3).

For elegant dining, make a reservation at **Garden Restaurant** (tel. 506/2645-5057, 6am-8:20am, noon-2pm, and 6pm-8:30pm daily), at Monteverde Lodge, which dishes up superb gourmet cuisine. A typical dinner might include shredded duck empanadas ($6), roasted leek quiche ($8.50), and entrées of almond chicken curry with rice in a coconut cup ($13), followed by profiteroles ($7). It has a large wine list.

For fusion cuisine, make a beeline to ★ **Sofia** (tel. 506/2645-7017, knielsenmv@hotmail.com, 11:30am-9:30pm daily) in Cerro Plano, which serves gourmet Nuevo Latino dishes. Chef-owner Karen Nielsen whips up mean appetizers, such as a roasted eggplant, tomato, and goat cheese quesadilla, and black bean soup. For a main course, try the seafood chimichanga ($12) or plantain-crusted sea bass ($12). The bar serves very good mojitos, caipirinhas, and other cocktails ($5). Sofia has wine tastings and occasionally hosts live music such as choral and jazz. Karen also operates the chic fusion restaurant **Trio** (tel. 506/2645-7254, 11:30am-9pm daily) in Santa Elena. Decked out with an urbane chocolate, pea-green, and white decor, it has huge windows and a deck with forest views. Try the cream of carrot and sweet potato soup with coconut and tamarind ($4), followed by mojito shrimp ($12.50).

Karen also runs a gourmet yet casual tapas restaurant, **Chimera** (tel. 506/2645-7017, 11:30am-9:30pm daily), with an open kitchen; it's perfect if you want to share plates or have a light appetite. Everything here is organically grown. Choice selections include cold roasted eggplant ($3.50), coconut shrimp lollipops with mango-ginger sauce ($7.50), and smoked provolone with sun-dried tomato sauce ($3.50).

Restaurante y Pizzería Tramonti (400

meters/0.25 miles uphill from the gas station in Monteverde, tel. 506/2645-6120, www.tramonticr.com, 11:30am-9:45pm daily) offers good ambience along with excellent spaghetti dishes, carpaccio, lasagna, fried squid, and wood-fired pizzas ($5-15). While we're talking Italian, Johnny's Pizzería (1 kilometer/0.6 miles east of Santa Elena, tel. 506/2645-5066, www.pizzeriadejohnny.com, 11:30am-9:30pm daily), in Cerro Plano, is both classy and offers a wide-ranging pizza menu (small-large $4-10) plus pastas and daily specials such as smoked salmon and capers. It also has a tapas bar with nightly live music.

For a chocolaty treat or a delicious light lunch head to ★ Café Caburé (tel. 506/2645-5020, www.cabure.net, 8am-8pm Mon.-Sat.), at Paseo de Estella. Argentinean owner Susana Salas's eclectic menu offers chocolate-inspired dishes and drinks from around the world. You must try the passion fruit-, rum-, and vodka-flavored truffles. Salas also serves gourmet organic salads and wraps ($9.50). Caburé has Wi-Fi plus an excellent chocolate museum. Craving ice cream? Head to Heladería Monteverde (tel. 506/2645-6558, 10am-8pm daily), run by the cheese factory and serving 20 flavors of ice cream, such as blackberry and cherry. It's in the heart of Santa Elena.

INFORMATION AND SERVICES

The best starting point for visitor information is the impartial Chamber of Commerce (tel. 506/2645-6565, www.visitmonteverde.com, 8am-8pm daily) and, across the street, the Monteverde Information Center (tel. 506/2645-6559). Both are located in the center of Santa Elena. Desafío Tours (tel. 506/2645-5874, www.monteverdetours.com), in Santa Elena, also books tours and offers visitor advice. The Monteverde Conservation League (tel. 506/2645-5003, www.acmcr.org, 8am-5pm Mon.-Fri., 8am-noon Sat.), mid-way between Santa Elena and the Monteverde Cloud Forest Biological Reserve, is a great resource for information on ecological projects and the reserves.

The state-run Centro Médico Monteverde (tel. 506/2645-7080) clinic is on the west side of Santa Elena. In Cerro Plano, the Consultorio Médico (tel. 506/2645-7778, 24 hours daily) has a clinic and an ambulance. The Red Cross (tel. 506/2645-6128) is on the north side of Santa Elena. A private dental clinic (tel. 506/2645-7080) adjoins the post office.

The police (Guardia Rural, tel. 911 or 506/2645-6248) faces Super La Esperanza in Santa Elena. The Banco Nacional (tel. 506/2645-5027), in Santa Elena, is open 8:30am-3:30pm daily. The post office is on the east side of Santa Elena.

For Internet access, head to Treehouse Internet (tel. 506/2645-5751, 6am-11pm daily), or Internet Pura Vida (tel. 506/2645-5783, 10am-8pm daily), which also has laundry. Las Delicias Campesinas (tel. 506/2645-7032), in Cerro Plano, has self-service laundry ($6 per load).

The Centro Panamericano de Idiomas (50 meters/165 feet west of the gas station in Monteverde, tel./fax 506/2645-5441, www.cpi-edu.com) offers Spanish-language courses at its impressive facility. The Monteverde Institute (tel. 506/2645-5053, www.mvinstitute.org) hosts one-week arts workshops at the Monteverde Studios of the Arts (June-Aug.).

GETTING THERE AND AROUND

Beware touts who intercept arriving buses and cars to direct you to properties or businesses at which they'll receive commissions.

Transportes Monteverde (tel. 506/2645-5159, San José tel. 506/2222-3854) buses depart San José (4 hours, $5) from Calle 12, Avenidas 7/9, at 6:30am and 2:30pm daily; return buses depart Santa Elena at 6:30am and 2:30pm daily. The office in Santa Elena is open 5:45am-11:30am daily, as well as 1:30pm-5pm Monday-Friday and 1:30pm-3pm Saturday-Sunday. Buy your return bus ticket as soon as you arrive in Santa Elena. Buses also depart Calles 2/4 in Puntarenas at 7:50am, 1:50pm,

Between Monteverde and La Fortuna

For many travelers in Monteverde, the next destination of choice is La Fortuna (or vice versa). There are several ways of traveling between them. Most popular is a four-hour horseback ride from Monteverde to Río Chiquito, where you take a one-hour boat ride across Laguna de Arenal, then a 30-minute Jeep ride to La Fortuna. There are three different routes for the horseback ride. Several tour operators compete. Some have been accused of working their horses to death—literally—on the arduous San Gerardo Trail, on which horses that are often poorly fed exhaust themselves struggling through thigh-deep mud on the steep hills during wet season. The Río Chiquito route can also be tough on horses in wet season. The Lake Trail is the easiest on the horses. Check to see that the horses are not used both ways on the same day.

Alternatively, you can take a 90-minute Jeep ride to Río Chiquito, then continue on the one-hour boat ride across Laguna de Arenal and a 30-minute Jeep ride to La Fortuna.

and 2:15pm daily (you can pick it up at the Río Lagarto turnoff for Monteverde on the Pan-American Hwy.) and depart Monteverde at 4:30am, 6am, and 3pm daily. A bus departs Tilarán for Monteverde at 12:30pm daily, returning from Monteverde at 7am daily.

Interbus (tel. 506/4100-0888, www.interbusonline.com) and **Grayline Costa Rica** (tel. 506/2220-2393, www.graylinecostarica.com) operate shuttles between San José and Monteverde ($35) and key tourist destinations.

If you're *driving,* there are two turnoffs for Monteverde from Highway 1. The first is via Sardinal; the turnoff is at Rancho Grande, about 10 kilometers (6 miles) south of San Gerardo. The second is about seven kilometers (4.5 miles) north of San Gerardo (100 meters/330 feet before the bridge over the Río Lagarto), 37 kilometers (23 miles) north of Esparza. The roads lead 35 kilometers (22 miles) uphill along a gut-jolting dirt road as famous as the place it leads to. The drive takes 1.5 to 2 hours.

There is no local bus service except to the Reserva Biológica Bosque Nuboso Monteverde.

TILARÁN

Tilarán, about 23 kilometers (14 miles) east of Cañas and the Pan-American Highway, is the western gateway to Lake Arenal and Monteverde. This spruce little highland town is laid out in a grid around a pretty square and a park with cedars and pines in front of the small cathedral, **Catedral de San Antonio,** which has an amazing barrel-vaulted wooden ceiling. At 550 meters (1,800 feet) elevation, the air is crisp and stirred by breezes working their way over the crest of the Cordillera de Tilarán from Laguna de Arenal, five kilometers (3 miles) to the northeast. The countryside hereabouts is reminiscent of the rolling hill country of England.

The last weekend in April, Tilarán hosts a rodeo and a livestock show. On June 13, Tilarán celebrates San Antonio, the patron saint, with a bullfight and a rodeo.

Cataratas de Viento Fresco (tel. 506/2695-3434, www.vientofresco.net, 7:30am-5pm daily, adults $15, students $12), 11 kilometers (7 miles) east of Tilarán on the rough dirt road to Monteverde, has four 37-meter (120-foot) waterfalls, a waterslide, trails, and horseback riding ($55).

Accommodations and Food

A recommended bargain, **Hotel El Sueño** (tel. 506/2695-5347, standard $22 s, $32 d, deluxe $28 s, $38 d), one block north of the plaza, is a charming no-frills budget option. Sixteen rooms, all with TVs, fans, and hot water, surround a sunlit second-floor courtyard with fountain. Four more deluxe rooms have fridges and somewhat more ostentatious furnishings. The friendly owners provide fruit and toiletry baskets. Downstairs, the Restaurant El Parque has good seafood dishes. It has secure parking.

Understandably popular with tour groups, **Aroma Tico** (tel. 506/2695-3065, 6:30am-9:30pm daily), at the main entrance to town (the junction for Cañas and Laguna de Arenal), is a top choice for its clean ambience, hearty Tico fare, bargain buffet, and an excellent selection of souvenirs. Go on Sunday afternoon for live marimba music.

Information and Services

There are banks around the town square, which has public phones. **Café Internet Tica Explorer** (8:30am-10pm daily) is two blocks northeast of the plaza.

The **Red Cross** (tel. 506/2695-5256) is one block east of the church, and **Clínica Tilarán** (tel. 506/2695-5115) is open 24 hours daily. The **police station** (tel. 506/2695-5001) adjoins the bus station, 100 meters (330 feet) northwest of the plaza.

Getting There and Around

Auto Transportes Tilarán (tel. 506/2256-0105) buses depart San José (via Cañas, 4 hours, $3) from Calle 20, Avenida 3, at 7:30am, 9:30am, 12:45pm, 3:45pm, and 6:30pm daily. The bus continues to Nuevo Arenal. Local buses depart Cañas five times daily for Tilarán 5am-1:45pm; from La Fortuna at 8am and 4:30pm daily; from Santa Elena (Monteverde, tel. 506/2695-3102) at 4:30am and 12:30pm daily; and from Puntarenas at 11:45am and 4:30pm daily. Buses depart Tilarán for San José at 5am, 7am, 9:30am, 2pm, and 5pm daily; for Cañas six times 5am-3:30pm daily; for La Fortuna at 7am and 12:30pm daily; for Monteverde at 7am and 4pm daily; and for Puntarenas at 6am and 1pm daily.

There's a **gas station** two blocks northeast of the plaza. For taxis call **Unidos Tilarán** (tel. 506/2695-5324), or hail one on the west side of the plaza.

Cañas and Vicinity

As you continue northwest along Highway 1 from Cañas, the first impression is of a vast barren plain, burning hot in dry season, with palms rising like tattered umbrellas over the scrubby landscape, flanked to the east by the steep-sided volcanoes of the Cordillera de Guanacaste, from which rivers feed the marshy wetlands of the Tempisque Basin. Away from the main highway, the villages of whitewashed houses are as welcoming as any in the country. For the traveler interested in history or architecture, there are some intriguing sights, and the area is charged with scenic beauty.

CAÑAS

Cañas is a modest-size town and a pivotal point for exploring Parque Nacional Palo Verde (west) or Laguna de Arenal (east), and

for rafting trips on the Río Corobicí. Named for the white-flowered wild cane that still grows in patches hereabouts, Cañas is indisputably a cowboy town, as the many tanned *sabaneros* riding horses and shaded by wide-brimmed hats attest. Note the **Monumento a los Boyeros** (Ave. 5 and Hwy. 1), dedicated to yesteryear's oxcart drivers. Worth a stop is the main church—the **Parroquia de Cañas** (on the main plaza)—with its facade entirely inlaid with mosaic, the work of local conceptual artist Otto Apuy, who has graced the interior with psychedelic murals, including rainforest-themed stained-glass windows.

A paved road runs west from Cañas 14 kilometers (9 miles) to the village of Bebedero, a gateway to Parque Nacional Palo Verde; there's no bridge, but boats will take passengers across the wide Río Tenorio.

Cañas

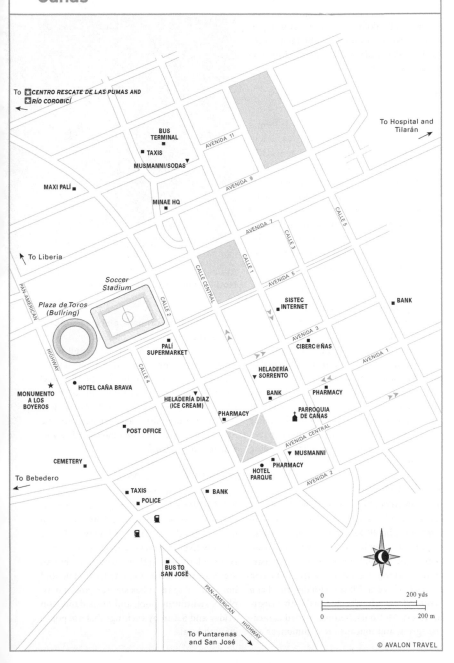

To ✚CENTRO RESCATE DE LAS PUMAS AND
✚RÍO COROBICÍ

To Hospital and
Tilarán

BUS
TERMINAL

AVENIDA 11

TAXIS
MUSMANNI/SODAS

MAXI PALÍ

AVENIDA 9

MINAE HQ

CALLE 5

AVENIDA 7

CALLE 3

To Liberia

Soccer
Stadium

CALLE 1

AVENIDA 5

CALLE CENTRAL

Plaza de Toros
(Bullring)

CALLE 2

SISTEC
INTERNET

BANK

PAN-AMERICAN

HIGHWAY

AVENIDA 3

PALÍ
SUPERMARKET

CIBERC@ÑAS

AVENIDA 1

CALLE 4

HELADERÍA
SORRENTO

MONUMENTO
A LOS
BOYEROS

HOTEL CAÑA BRAVA

HELADERÍA DIAZ
(ICE CREAM)

BANK

PHARMACY

PHARMACY

PARROQUIA
DE CAÑAS

POST OFFICE

AVENIDA CENTRAL

CEMETERY

MUSMANNI

To Bebedero

HOTEL
PARQUE

PHARMACY

AVENIDA 2

TAXIS
POLICE

BANK

BUS TO
SAN JOSÉ

0   200 yds

0   200 m

PAN-AMERICAN

HIGHWAY

To Puntarenas
and San José

© AVALON TRAVEL

Seven kilometers (4.5 miles) north of Cañas and one kilometer (0.6 miles) north of the Río Corobicí, a well-paved road, Highway 6, leads northeast 58 kilometers (36 miles) to Upala in the northern lowlands via Bijagua, in the low-lying saddle of the Tenorio and Miravalles volcanoes.

★ Centro de Rescate Las Pumas

Centro de Rescate Las Pumas (Las Pumas Rescue Center, tel. 506/2669-6044, www. centrorescatelaspumas.org, 8am-4pm daily, adults $10, students and children $5), five kilometers (3 miles) north of Cañas, was founded by the late Lilly Bodmer de Hagnauer, a Swiss-born environmentalist whose passion was saving and raising big cats: ocelots, jaguars, cougars, margays, jaguarundis, and oncillas (tiger cats). All six species are housed in large chain-link cages, but beware—there are no guardrails (nor guards), and the temptation to reach out to stroke a cat through the mesh is tempting but ill-advised. These are not house cats! Most of the animals were either injured or orphaned and have been reared by Lilly or her family, who still run the zoo. Those that can be released to the wild are rehabilitated in an area closed to the public.

Other species include deer, foxes, monkeys, peccaries, macaws, toucans, and dozens of parrots and other birds. The center also raises rabbits for sale. By selling only nonnative species, it hopes to help change the pet-keeping habits of Ticos.

★ Río Corobicí

Six kilometers (4 miles) north of Cañas, the Pan-American Highway crosses the Río Corobicí. The 40-kilometer-long (25-mile-long) river is fed by controlled runoff from Laguna de Arenal, providing water year-round, making it good for rafting. The trip is a relatively calm Class II run described as a "nature float." The river is lined with a riparian forest. Motmots, herons, crested caracaras, egrets, and toucans are common, as are

Mosaics adorn the Parroquia de Cañas.

howler monkeys, caimans, and iguanas basking on the riverbanks.

Safaris Corobicí (tel. 506/2669-6191, www.nicoya.com) has an office beside Highway 1, about 400 meters (0.25 miles) south of the river. It has guided floats on the river ($37-60), as does **Ríos Tropicales** (www. riostropicales.com), based at Restaurante Rincón Corobicí (tel. 506/2669-6262, www. rinconcorobici.com).

Accommodations and Food

You can camp at the budget **Hotel Capazuri** (tel. 506/2669-6280, camping $12 pp, rooms $25 pp), two kilometers (1.2 miles) north of town, on the east side of Highway 1. The friendly live-in owners rent out 19 rooms in two modern blocks; they vary in size, but all are clean and simply furnished, with fans and hot water. Capazuri has showers and toilets, plus a swimming pool, and hosts dances on Friday and Saturday evenings that are popular with locals.

Combining the atmosphere of a venerable cattle hacienda (which it is) and a stylish modern hotel, **Hacienda La Pacífica** (tel. 506/2669-6050, www.pacificacr.com, low season $53-59 s/d, high season $66-96 s/d, including breakfast) plays up its historic ambience in spacious rooms with high ceilings, wrought-iron candelabras, and huge colonial-style oak closets. Rooms have cable TV, Wi-Fi, and lovely modern baths. Alas, the mattresses and pillows are truly awful. But the delightfully rustic restaurant (7am-9pm daily, $5-15) serves an eclectic menu that includes cream of tomato soup, pastas, and tenderloin pepper steak. Most dishes are served with organic rice grown on the hacienda.

Restaurante Rincón Corobicí (tel. 506/2669-6262, www.rinconcorobici.com, 8am-6pm daily), beside the Pan-American Highway, is a pleasant place to eat, with good seafood dishes and a porch over the river where you can watch rafters go by. It prepares an excellent sea bass in garlic ($10); wash it down with superb lemonade.

You can't miss the huge signs on the Pan-American Highway advertising **Bar-B-Q Tres Hermanas** (tel. 506/2662-8584, www.bbqtreshermanas.com, 7am-9pm daily), about 20 kilometers (12 miles) south of town. Carnivores will devour the marinated and slow-grilled chicken, pork, and beef.

Information and Services

The **Comité de Cultura** (tel. 506/2669-0042), in the Edificio Palacio Municipal, on the north side of the main plaza, has visitor information. There are banks in the town center. The **post office** is on Avenida 3, about 30 meters (100 feet) west of Calle 4. The **police station** (tel. 506/2669-0057) is two kilometers (1.2 miles) south of town.

Internet Cibercañas (Ave. 3, Calles 1/3, tel. 506/2669-5232) is open 8:15am-9pm Monday-Saturday, 2pm-9pm Sunday. The **MINAE National Park Service headquarters** (tel. 506/2669-0533) is on Avenida 9, Calle Central.

Getting There

Empresa La Cañera (tel. 506/2258-5792) buses depart San José (3 hours, $3) for Cañas from Calle 14, Avenidas 1/3, five times daily 7:30am-6:30pm. **Empresa Reina del Campo** (tel. 506/2663-1752) buses depart Liberia nine times daily. Buses depart Cañas for San José from Calle 1, Avenidas 9/11, five times daily 5:30am-5pm.

Taxis Unidos de Cañas (tel. 506/2669-0898) has taxis on call.

MIRAVALLES VOLCANO

The small, nondescript town of Bagaces is on Highway 1, about 22 kilometers (14 miles) north of Cañas. Bagaces is the gateway to Parque Nacional Palo Verde (west) and Volcán Miravalles (east).

Highway 164 leads northeast from Bagaces and climbs steadily up the western shoulder of Volcán Miravalles (2,028 meters/6,654 feet), enshrined within the **Zona Protectora Miravalles** (Miravalles Protected Zone). The almost perfectly conical volcano is the highest in the Cordillera de Guanacaste. The western slopes are covered with savanna scrub; the northern and eastern slopes are lush, fed by moist clouds that sweep in from the Caribbean. The southern slopes are cut with deep canyons and licked by ancient lava tongues, with fumaroles spouting and hissing like mini Old Faithfuls. The forests, replete with wildlife, are easily accessed from the road. There are no developed trails or facilities for visitors, however, and no ranger station.

Highway 164 runs via the village of **Guayabo,** 21 kilometers (13 miles) north of Bagaces (it has a bank, an Internet café, and several *cabinas*). It is paved as far as **Aguas Claras** and extends beyond to the hamlet of San José in the northern lowlands. If you're souvenir shopping, call in at **Galería Tony Jiménez** (tel. 506/8821-8358, www.tonyjimenez.com), midway between Guayabo and Aguas Claras.

A loop road from Highway 164 leads east via the community of **La Fortuna de**

Bagaces to Las Hornillas (Little Ovens), an area of intensely bubbling mud pots and fumaroles expelling foul gases and steam. Here the Costa Rican Institute of Electricity (ICE) harnesses geothermal energy for electric power, with two plants that tap the superheated vapor deep within the volcano's bowels. You can visit the main geothermal plant, Planta Miravalles (tel. 506/2673-1111, ext. 232), about two kilometers (1.2 miles) north of Fortuna, by appointment.

★ Las Hornillas Volcanic Activity Center

The prime spot to enjoy the volcanic activity is the mesmerizing Las Hornillas Volcanic Activity Center (tel. 506/8839-9769, www. hornillas.com, 8am-5pm daily, $35), a "walkable live crater" two kilometers (1.2 miles) southeast of the ICE geothermal plant. Boardwalks lead through the crater itself, with mud pools and fumaroles hissing and bubbling all around. You can walk around at will and even take a therapeutic bath in warm mud, while a two-hour guided tour ($45) includes a tractor tour to waterfalls. A highlight is the 100-meter-long (330-foot-long) waterslide. It recently added three pedestrian swing bridges. It has showers and toilets, plus four cabins ($50 s, $100 d, including unlimited use of the facility).

★ Río Perdido Activity Center

"Wow" was my first reaction on seeing the deluxe Río Perdido Activity Center (tel. 506/2673-3600, www.rioperdido.com, 9am-5pm daily), which opened in 2013 in a previously unexplored river valley on the southern slopes of Volcán Miravalles. In fact, the name Río Perdido (Lost River) refers to its remote location near the hamlet of San Bernardo de Bagaces, northeast of Bagaces. It encompasses a 200-hectare (500-acre) semideciduous forest reserve atop the Río Blanco canyon, framed by 46-meter (150-foot) soaring rock walls.

At its core is a very sophisticated restaurant and spa, with stunning contemporary architecture and panoramic views through a curvilinear floor-to-ceiling wall of glass overlooking a swimming pool—one of three that grace the property. Gourmet nouvelle dining is strongly influenced by traditional Guanacastecan cuisine, courtesy of chef Andrés Flores, who is also a champion downhill biker. In fact, the center is billed not least as a bike park. Flores helped design the 19-kilometer (12-mile) network of dedicated bike trails ($12) that is a highlight of Río Perdido.

thermal swimming pool at Río Perdido Activity Center

You can also rent bicycles ($30-40) with advance notice, or sign up for a guided tour. Visitors also get to thrill to white-water rafting on the Río Blanco, or tubing on the Río Cuipilapa. The canyon is a setting for adrenaline-inducing aerial zip lines and Tarzan swing ("Canyon Adventure," $48). Plus you can go tubing ($40). The center's coup de grâce is probably its chic full-service spa for soothing away any aches after all the activity.

Accommodations and Food

The no-frills **Centro Turístico Yökö** (tel. 506/2673-0410, www.yokotermales.com, $40 s, $60 d) has 12 spacious, simply furnished, and perfectly comfortable cabins with verandas with volcano views, plus ceiling fans and large walk-in showers with hot spring water. It has a restaurant with a TV. Rates include breakfast and use of the facilities.

★ **Río Perdido Activity Center** (tel. 506/2673-3600, www.rioperdido.com, low season $200 s/d, high season $220 s/d) will delight sophisticates who appreciate fine contemporary taste. Its 20 stupendously stylish, postmodernist, modular, steel-shell bungalows are a city-slickers delight with glazed concrete floors, stainless steel highlights, glass walls, and lively yet calming Ikea-style

furnishings, plus decks with hammocks. They're set well apart amid the dry forest, plus you get the superb restaurant, spa, and other facilities at hand.

Information and Services

A good resource is the **Cámara de Turismo Tenorio-Miravalles** (tel. 506/2466-8221, 9am-3pm daily), the local Chamber of Tourism, on the south side of Bijagua.

Getting There

Buses (tel. 506/2221-3318) for Guayabo depart San José from Calle 12, Avenidas 3/5, at 5:30am and 2pm daily and travel via Bagaces.

★ PALO VERDE NATIONAL PARK

Parque Nacional Palo Verde ($10), 28 kilometers (17 miles) south of Bagaces, protects 13,058 hectares (32,267 acres) of floodplain, marshes, and seasonal pools in the heart of the driest region of Costa Rica—the Tempisque basin, at the mouth of the Río Tempisque in the Golfo de Nicoya. The park derives its name from the *palo verde* (green stick) shrub that retains its bright green coloration year-round.

For half the year—November to March—no

mountain biker at Río Perdido Activity Center

rain relieves the heat of the Tempisque basin, leaving plants and trees parched and withered. Rolling, rocky terrain spared what is now the Lomas Barbudal reserve, in particular, from the changes wrought on the rest of Guanacaste Province by plows and cows. Here, the dry forest that once extended along the entire Pacific coast of Mesoamerica remains largely intact, and several endangered tree species thrive, such as Panamá redwood, rosewood, sandbox, and the *balas de cañón* (cannonball tree). A relative of the Brazil nut tree, the cannonball tree produces a pungent, nonedible fruit that grows to the size of a bowling ball and dangles from a long stem. Several evergreen tree species also line the banks of the waterways, creating riparian corridors inhabited by species not usually found in dry forests.

In all, there are 15 different habitats and a corresponding diversity of fauna. Plump crocodiles wallow on the muddy riverbanks, salivating, no doubt, at the sight of coatis, white-tailed deer, and other mammals that come down to the water to drink.

white ibis, Palo Verde National Park

Parque Nacional Palo Verde is best known as a bird-watchers' paradise. More than 300 bird species have been recorded, not least great curassows and the only permanent colony of scarlet macaws in the dry tropics. At least 250,000 wading birds and waterfowl flock here in fall and winter, when much of the arid alluvial plain swells into a lake. Isla de Pájaros, in the middle of the Río Tempisque, is replete with white ibis, roseate spoonbills, anhingas, wood storks, jabiru storks, and the nation's largest colony of black-crowned night herons.

Three well-maintained trails lead to lookout points over the lagoons; to limestone caves; and to water holes such as Laguna Bocana, gathering places for a diversity of birds and animals. Limestone cliffs rise behind the old Hacienda Palo Verde, now the **park headquarters** (tel. 506/2200-0125, www.actempisque.webs.com or www.sinac. go.cr), eight kilometers (5 miles) south of the park entrance.

Dry season (Nov.–Apr.) is by far the best time to visit, although the Tempisque basin can get dizzyingly hot. Access is easier at this time of year, and deciduous trees lose their leaves, making bird-watching easier. Wildlife gathers by the water holes, and there are far fewer mosquitoes and other bugs. When the rains come, mosquitoes burst into action.

The park is contiguous to the north with the remote 7,354-hectare (18,172-acre) **Refugio de Fauna Silvestre Rafael Lucas Rodríguez Caballero,** a wildlife refuge, and beyond that, the 2,279-hectare (5,632-acre) **Reserva Biológica Lomas Barbudal** (Lomas Barbudal Biological Reserve, no tel., www.sinac.go.cr, donation). The three have a similar variety of habitats. The Lomas Barbudal park office (Casa de Patrimonio) is on the banks of the Río Cabuyo. Trails span the park from here. It's open on a 10-days-open, 4-days-closed schedule.

To the south, Parque Nacional Palo Verde is contiguous with **Refugio de Vida Silvestre Cipancí** (tel. 506/2651-8115), a national wildlife refuge that protects mangroves in 3,500 square kilometers (1,350 square miles) of riverside bordering the Ríos Tempisque and Bebedero. The banks of the Tempisque, which is tidal, are lined with archaeological sites.

Recreation

The **Organization of Tropical Studies** (OTS, tel. 506/2661-4717, www.ots.ac.cr) offers natural-history visits by advance reservation; guided walks cost $28-65, depending on the number of people. It also has birding and nocturnal walks ($30-80), plus boat tours ($45-57).

Tour companies in San José and throughout Guanacaste also offer river tours in Palo Verde, including **Aventuras Arenal** (tel. 506/2479-9133, www.aventurasarenal. com) from Bebedero. You can also explore Palo Verde from the Nicoya side of the Río Tempisque with **Palo Verde Boat Tours** (tel. 506/2651-8001, www.paloverdeboattours.com), departing Filadelfia and from **Hacienda El Viejo** (tel. 506/2665-7759, www. elviejowetlands.com), 17 kilometers (11 miles) southeast of Filadelfia.

Accommodations

The Parque Nacional Palo Verde administration building has a run-down campsite ($2) beside the old Hacienda Palo Verde. Water, showers, and barbecue pits are available. There is also a campsite seven kilometers (4.5 miles) east near Laguna Coralillo (no facilities). It is periodically closed, so call ahead to check. You may be able to stay with rangers in basic accommodations ($12) with advance notice; for information call the **Área de Conservación Tempisque** office (tel. 506/2695-5908, 8am-4pm daily) in Tilarán. Spanish-speakers might try the ranger station radio phone (tel. 506/2233-4160).

Visitors can also stay in a dormitory at the Organization of Tropical Studies' **Palo Verde Biological Research Station** (tel. 506/2661-4717, www.ots.ac.cr, reservations tel. 506/2524-0607, reservas@ots.ac.cr, low season $77 s, $148 d, high season $93 s, $186 d, including meals and a guided walk) on a

space-available basis. Eight rooms have shared baths; five rooms have private baths.

The Reserva Biológica Lomas Barbudal has basic accommodations ($6 pp) and meals at the ranger station.

Information

The **Área de Conservación Arenal-Tempisque** (ACT, tel. 506/2671-1290, www. acarenaltempisque.org, 8am-4pm Mon.-Fri.) regional national parks office is opposite the junction for Palo Verde, next to the gas station on Highway 1, at the entrance to Bagaces.

Getting There

The main entrance to Parque Nacional Palo Verde is 28 kilometers (17 miles) south of Bagaces, along a dirt road that begins opposite the gas station and Área de Conservación Tempisque office on Highway 1. The route is signed; a 4WD vehicle is required, and high ground clearance is essential in wet season. No buses travel this route. A **Jeep taxi** from Bagaces costs about $30 one-way.

Coming from the Nicoya Peninsula, a **bus** operates from the town of Nicoya to Puerto Humo, where you can hire a boat to take you three kilometers (2 miles) upriver to the Chamorro dock, the trailhead to park headquarters; it's a two-kilometer (1.2-mile) walk, and it's muddy and swampy in wet season. Alternatively, you can **drive** from Filadelfia or Santa Cruz (on the Nicoya Peninsula) to Hacienda El Viejo; the park is four kilometers (2.5 miles) east from El Viejo, and the Río Tempisque two kilometers (1.2 miles) farther. A local boat operator will ferry you downriver to the Chamorro dock.

The unpaved access road for Reserva Biológica Lomas Barbudal is off Highway 1, at the Km. 221 marker near Pijijes, about 10 kilometers (6 miles) north of Bagaces. A dirt road—4WD recommended—leads six kilometers (4 miles) to a lookout point and then descends steeply from here to the park entrance. If conditions are particularly muddy, you can park at the lookout point and hike to the ranger station rather than face not being able to return via the dauntingly steep ascent from the ranger station in your vehicle. A Jeep taxi from Bagaces will cost about $50 round-trip. Palo Verde and Lomas Barbudal are also linked by a rough dirt road that is tough going in wet season.

Liberia and Vicinity

LIBERIA

Liberia, 26 kilometers (16 miles) north of Bagaces, is the provincial capital. It is also one of the country's most intriguing historic cities, with charming colonial structures made of blinding white ignimbrite, for which it is called the "white city." Many old adobe homes still stand to the south of the landscaped central plaza, with high-ceilinged interiors and kitchens opening onto classical courtyards. Old corner houses have doors—*puertas del sol*—that open on two sides to catch both morning and afternoon sun. Many of the historic houses along **Calle Real** (Calle Central, Aves. Central/8) have been restored, and at press time the street was due to be pedestrianized. The most interesting house is **Casa del Papel** (tel. 506/2666-0626), at the corner of Avenida 4, entirely covered with newspapers.

The leafy plaza hosts a modernist church—**Iglesia Inmaculada Concepción de María**—and a colonial-era town hall flying the Guanacastecan flag. On the square's northwest corner, the old city jail, with towers at each corner, has metamorphosed into the **Museo de Guanacaste** (tel. 506/2665-7114, 8am-4pm Mon.-Sat., free). Still a work in progress, its contemporary interior has art spaces and performance venues.

At the far end of Avenida Central (also known as Ave. 25 Julio) is the recently restored **La Ermita La Agonía** (tel. 506/2666-0107, 2:30pm-3:30pm daily, other times by request, free). Dating from 1854, the church has a stucco exterior, simple adornments, and a small **Religious Art Museum.**

The town has long been a center for the local cattle industry. A **statue** at Avenida Central and Calle 10 honors the *sabaneros* (cowboys). The **Museo de Sabanero** (tel. 506/2666-0135, no set hours, by donation),

colonial-era building on Calle Real, Liberia

Liberia

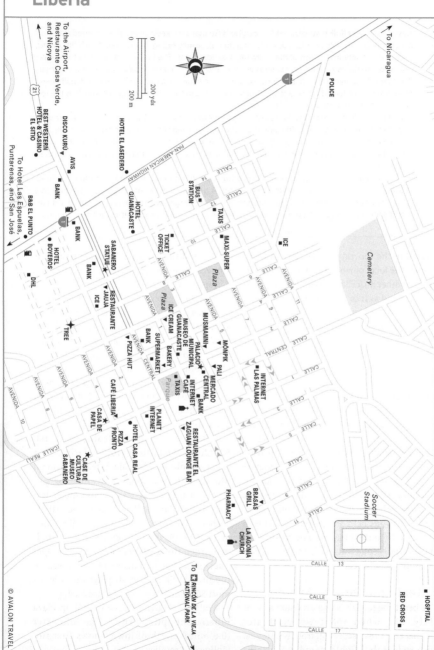

To Nicaragua

POLICE

To the Airport,
Restaurante Casa Verde,
and Nicoya

21

BESTWESTERN
HOTEL & CASINO
EL SITIO

DISCO KURÚ

AVIS

BANK

B&B EL PUNTO

To Hotel Las Espuelas,
Puntarenas, and San José

HOTEL
BOTEROS

DHL

HOTEL EL ASEDERO

PAN-AMERICAN HIGHWAY

HOTEL
GUANACASTE

BANK

SABANERO
STATUE

BANK

RESTAURANTE
JAUA

ICE

TREE

BUS
STATION

TAXIS

TICKET
OFFICE

MAXI-SUPER

Plaza

Plaza

ICE CREAM

BAKERY

BANK

SUPERMARKET

PIZZA HUT

CAFÉ LIBERIA

CASA DE
PAPEL

CASE DE
CULTURA/
MUSEO
SABANERO

MUSMANNI

MUSEO DE
GUANACASTE

PALACIO
MUNICIPAL

MONPIK

PALI

MERCADO
CENTRAL

INTERNET
CAFÉ

BANK

TAXIS

PLANET
INTERNET

PIZZA
PRONTO

HOTEL CASA REAL

ICE

INTERNET
LAS PALMAS

Cemetery

RESTAURANTE EL
ZAGUAN LOUNGE BAR

PHARMACY

BRASAS
GRILL

LA AGONIA
CHURCH

Soccer
Stadium

To
RINCÓN DE LA VIEJA
NATIONAL PARK

CALLE 13

CALLE 15

CALLE 17

HOSPITAL

RED CROSS

Parque

CALLE 14

CALLE 12

CALLE 10

AVENIDA 3

AVENIDA

AVENIDA 5

AVENIDA 1

AVENIDA

AVENIDA CENTRAL

AVENIDA 2

AVENIDA 4

AVENIDA 6

AVENIDA 8

AVENIDA 10

CALLE REAL

CALLE 11

CALLE 9

CALLE 7

CALLE 5

CALLE 3

CALLE CENTRAL

CALLE 2

CALLE 1

CALLE 9

CALLE 11

0   200 yds
0   200 m

© AVALON TRAVEL

Costa Rican Rodeo

Fiestas populares (folk festivals), held throughout Guanacaste, keep alive a deep-rooted tradition of Costa Rican culture: *recorridos de toros* (bull riding), bronco riding, home-style Tico bullfighting, and *topes*, or demonstrations of the Costa Rican saddle horse. The bulls are enraged before being released into the ring, where *vaqueteros* are on hand to distract the wild and dangerous animals if a rider is thrown or injured. (Their title comes from *vaqueta*, a piece of leather originally used by cowboys on haciendas to make stubborn bulls move in the direction desired, much as the red cape is used by Spanish matadors.)

Cowboys ride bareback and hang onto angry, jumping, twisting bulls with only one hand (or "freestyle"—with no hands), although the *vaqueta* has given way to a red cloth (called a *capote* or *muleta*) or even the occasional clown. The *recorridos* also feature "best bull" competitions and incredible displays of skill—such as *sabaneros* (cowboys) who lasso bulls with their backs turned to the animals.

The events are a grand excuse for inebriation. As more and more beer is consumed, it fuels bravado, and scores of Ticos pour into the ring. A general melee ensues as Ticos try to prove their manhood by running past the bull, which is kept enraged with an occasional prod from an electric fork or a sharp instrument. The bull is never killed, but it's a pathetic sight nonetheless.

housed in the venerable Casa de la Cultura, honors the local cowboy tradition with saddles and other miscellaneous antiquities, scattered around as if in an attic. The building is a perfect example of a simple Liberian home with doors. It's maintained by volunteers of the Grupo Associación para la Cultura de Liberia.

Africa Safari Adventure Park

Guanacaste's savanna landscape is a perfect setting for **Africa Safari Adventure Park** (tel. 506/2666-1111, www.africasafaricostarica.com, 8am-6pm daily, adults $50, children $25), formerly Africa Mía, a private wildlife reserve at El Salto, nine kilometers (5.5 miles) south of Liberia. Elands, camels, ostriches, and zebras kick up dust alongside antelopes, giraffes, warthogs, and other creatures. The tour is in an open-air safari Jeep or a tractor-pulled trailer. The facility includes a gorgeous waterfall, and a snorkeling option is offered.

Entertainment and Events

The best time to visit is **Día de Guanacaste** (July 25), when the town celebrates Guanacaste's 1812 secession from Nicaragua, with rodeos, bullfights, parades, marimba music, and firecrackers. A similar passion is stirred for the Semana Cultural, the first week of September.

The Best Western Hotel & Casino El Sitio has a small **casino** (tel. 506/2666-1211, 4pm-5am Mon.-Sat.). The **Disco Kurú** (tel. 506/2666-0769, cover $5), across the street, pulses Thursday-Saturday and has karaoke Monday-Wednesday. **Restaurante El Zaguán** (Ave. Central, Calle 1, tel. 506/2666-2456, 11:30am-10pm Mon.-Fri., 7:30am-10pm Sat.-Sun.) hosts live music, from traditional guitar to electronica.

Café Liberia (Calle Real, Ave. 4, tel. 506/2653-1660, 10am-10pm daily), in a 120-year-old building declared a National Monument, is a fabulous venue for poetry readings, dance classes, and music lessons. Bohemians will appreciate the artistic events at **Hidden Garden Art Gallery** (tel. 506/2667-0592 or 506/8386-6872, http://hiddengarden.thevanstonegroup.com, 9am-3pm Tues.-Sat.), five kilometers (3 miles) west of the airport. The gallery displays works by almost 50 local artists, some renowned.

Multicines (tel. 506/2665-1515), in Plaza Liberia Shopping Center, one kilometer (0.6 miles) south of town, shows first-run Hollywood movies.

TALABARTERÍA Y PELETERÍA

a saddlemaker store in Liberia

Accommodations

Backpackers and budget hounds will find the best bargain to be the lackluster **Hotel Guanacaste** (tel. 506/2666-0085, www.hi-guanacaste.com, dorms $8, private rooms $11-16 s, $26 d, including tax, 15 percent discount with HI card), affiliated with Hostelling International. Truckers prefer this popular option, with 27 simple dorms and private rooms with fans; some have private cold-water baths. There's table tennis, a restaurant, a TV lounge, Skype for free international calls, and secure parking. Camping ($5 pp) is available.

For comfort, opt for the **Best Western El Sitio Hotel & Casino** (tel. 506/2666-1211, U.S. tel. 800-780-7234, www.bestwestern.com, from $53 s/d), 150 meters (500 feet) west of Highway 1 on the road to Nicoya. This modern motel-type chain hotel has 52 predictably furnished rooms with private baths. There's a large swimming pool and a sundeck, plus a gift store and a tour desk.

For intimacy, the most appealing place is ★ **El Punto Bed & Breakfast** (tel.

506/2665-2986, www.elpuntohotel.com, $60 s, $70 d), occupying a former school on the Pan-American Highway, 200 meters (660 feet) south of the main junction. Here, former classrooms have cleverly metamorphosed into six quirky, studio-style air-conditioned rooms furnished in colorful minimalist Ikea style, with upstairs lofts (which can get warm) and patios with lounge chairs. Gorgeous private baths feature organic toiletries and lots of steaming hot water. A common room has cable TV and Wi-Fi.

Out near the airport, the snazzy five-story **Hotel Hilton Garden Inn** (tel. 506/2690-8888, http://hiltongardeninn1.hilton.com, from $109 s/d) fits the usual Hilton mold and is by far the most sophisticated and stylish hotel in the area. State-of-the-art amenities in the comfy rooms include 32-inch high-definition TVs. It has a swimming pool, a gym, and a business center.

Food

Liberia offers some tremendous options for dining, including **Restaurante Jauja** (tel. 506/2665-2061, www.restaurantejaujacr.com, 11am-11pm Mon.-Sat., 11am-11pm Sun.), with elegant rattan furnishings and an open patio with a huge tree. Go for the bargain-priced *plato ejecutivo* lunch ($5), nightly specials ($10) such as chicken salad, dorado with papaya sauce, and apple strudel with ice cream, and even sushi. It also has tremendous baked goods.

Taking Liberia into gourmet heights is ★ **Casa Verde** (tel. 506/2665-5037, 11am-9pm daily), alias The Greenhouse, in a dramatic modernist building two kilometers (1.2 miles) west of Liberia. This super-stylish restaurant boasts walls of glass, glazed concrete floors, and delicious fusion dishes, such as stroganoff ($13), baby-back ribs ($23), and Thai-style fish with curry coconut and onion ($13). For breakfast, how about pancakes, huevos rancheros, or a full Greenhouse breakfast ($10)? It even has a separate sushi bar and hosts a five-course dinner with live music on Friday nights. Fresh-squeezed juices are served in full carafes. The owners, Israel, from Venezuela, and Tanya, from New Zealand, have concocted a fantastic venue and in 2014 opened an equally chic adjoining lounge bar.

The best coffee shop around is **Café Liberia** (Calle Real, Ave. 4, tel. 506/2653-1660, 7am-10pm Mon.-Sat.), where new French owners serve delicious gourmet coffees in a treasure of a building; note the Raphael cherubs on the ceiling. It also serves a good ceviche and hosts live music.

Café Europa (tel. 506/2668-1081, www.panaleman.com, 6am-6pm daily), a German bakery two kilometers (1.2 miles) west of the airport, is a perfect spot to pick up succulent fresh-baked croissants, Danish pastries, pumpernickel breads, and much more. It has an airy spot to sit and munch, but it can get hot inside.

Information and Services
The **Red Cross** adjoins the **hospital** (Ave. 4, Calles Central/2, tel. 506/2666-0011). The **police station** (tel. 506/2666-5656) is on Avenida 1, one block west of the plaza. The **post office** is at Calle 8, Avenida 3.

The icy **Planet Internet** (Calle Central, Ave. Central/2, cell 506/2666-3737, 8am-10pm Mon.-Thurs., 8am-11pm Fri.-Sat.) charges $1 per hour. There's a **laundry** at Avenida Central, Calle 9.

Getting There and Around
SANSA (tel. 506/2229-4100, U.S./Canada tel. 877-767-2672, www.flysansa.com) and **Nature Air** (tel. 506/2299-6000, U.S. tel. 800-235-9272, www.natureair.com) offer scheduled daily service between San José and **Daniel Oduber Quirós International Airport** (LIR, tel. 506/2668-1032), 12 kilometers (7.5 miles) west of town. In addition to charter airlines, most major North American carriers have direct flights from the U.S. and Canada to Liberia. The airport has a bank as well as immigration (tel. 506/2668-1014) and customs (tel. 506/2668-1068) facilities.

Pulmitan (tel. 506/2222-1650) buses depart San José for Liberia (4 hours, $7) from Calle 24, Avenidas 5/7, hourly 6am-8pm daily. **Empresa Reina del Campo** (tel. 506/2663-1752) buses depart Puntarenas for Liberia (2.5 hours, $3) from the bus terminal nine times 5am-3pm daily. Buses from Nicoya and Santa Cruz depart for Liberia hourly 5am-8pm daily.

There are three gas stations at the junction of Highway 1 and Avenida Central.

To rent a car, I recommend **U-Save Car Rental** (tel. 506/2668-1516, www.usavecostarica.com), with an outlet near the airport. Several other car rental agencies are nearby. **Taxis** (tel. 506/2666-3330) gather at the northwest corner of the plaza, by the bus station, and at the airport.

★ RINCÓN DE LA VIEJA NATIONAL PARK
Parque Nacional Rincón de la Vieja, an active volcano in a period of relative calm, is the largest of five volcanoes that make up the Cordillera de Guanacaste. The volcano comprises nine separate craters, with dormant Santa María (1,916 meters/6,286 feet) the tallest; its crater harbors a forest-rimmed lake popular with tapirs. The main crater—Von Seebach—still steams; it features Linnet Bird Lagoon, to the southeast of the active volcano. Icy Lago Los Jilgueros lies between the two craters. The last serious eruption was in 1983, but the park occasionally closes temporarily due to volcanic activity. The national electricity company has a geothermal plant, **Planta Las Pailas,** just below the Las Pailas Ranger Station.

The 14,083-hectare (34,800-acre) Parque Nacional Rincón de la Vieja (www.sinac.go.cr) extends from 650 to 1,916 meters (2,133-6,286 feet) in elevation on both the Caribbean and Pacific flanks of the cordillera. The Pacific side has a distinct dry season (if you want to climb to the craters, Feb.-Apr. is best); by contrast, the Caribbean side is lush and wet year-round, with as much as 500 centimeters (200 inches) of rainfall annually on higher slopes. The park is known for its profusion of orchid species. More than 300 species of birds include quetzals, toucanets, the elegant trogon, three-wattled bellbirds, and the curassow. Mammals include cougars; howler, spider, and white-faced monkeys; and kinkajous, sloths, tapirs, tayras, and even jaguars.

Ranger Stations

There are two ranger stations, accessed by different routes from Liberia. The headquarters is at **Hacienda Santa María,** about 27 kilometers (17 miles) northeast of Liberia, which contains an exhibition room. The 19th-century farmstead was once owned by former U.S. president Lyndon B. Johnson, who sold it to the park service. However, the main access point to the park is the **Las Pailas Ranger Station** (tel. 506/2200-0399), on the southwestern flank of the volcano and from where the summit trail begins.

Hiking

The lower slopes can be explored along relatively easy trails that begin at, and connect, the two ranger stations. The **Sendero Encantado** leads through cloud forest full of *guaria morada* orchids (the national flower) and links with a 12-kilometer (7.5-mile) trail that continues to **Las Pailas** (The Cauldrons), 50 hectares (124 acres) of bubbling mud

volcanoes, boiling hot spring waters, vapor geysers, and **Las Hornillas fumaroles,** a geyser of sulfur dioxide and hydrogen sulfide. Be careful when walking around: It is possible to step through the crust and scald yourself, or worse.

Between the cloud forest and Las Pailas, a side trail (marked "Aguas Termales") leads to soothing hot-sulfur springs called **Los Azufrales** (The Sulfurs). The 42°C (108°F) hot spring waters form small pools where you may bathe and take advantage of their purported curative properties. Use the cold-water stream nearby for cooling off. Another trail leads to the **Hidden Waterfalls,** four continuous falls, three of which exceed 70 meters (230 feet), in the Agria Ravine.

You're restricted to hiking one trail at a time, and must report to the ranger station before setting out on each subsequent trail. If you don't report back, rangers set out to find you after a specified time.

The **summit hike** is relatively straightforward but challenging. You can do the round-trip to the summit and back in a day with a very early start. The trail begins at the Las Pailas Ranger Station (it's 4 hours from here), and snakes up the steep, scrubby mountainside. En route, you cross a bleak expanse of

hikers admiring a ficus, Rincón de la Vieja National Park

purple lava fossilized by the blitz of the sun. Trails are marked by cairns, though it is easy to get lost if the clouds set in; consider hiring a local guide. The upper slopes are of loose scree and very demanding.

It can be cool up here, but the powerful view and the hard, windy silence make for a profound experience. From on high, you have a splendid view of the wide Guanacaste plain shimmering in the heat like a dream world between hallucination and reality, and beyond, the mountains of Nicoya glisten like hammered gold from the sunlight slanting in from the south. On a clear day, you can see Gran Lago de Nicaragua. It's magical—you have only the sighing of the wind for company.

It will probably be cloudy. Bring waterproof clothing and mosquito repellent. The grasses harbor ticks and other biting critters, so wear long pants. Fill up with water at the ranger station, which sells maps ($2).

You must return the same day; no overnighting at the summit or along the trail is permitted. Be careful on your descent (3 hours).

Information and Services

The park is open 7am-5pm Tuesday-Sunday, and last entry is 3pm. Admission costs $10; you need to provide your passport number.

Camping is not permitted, except at Santa María Ranger Station ($2 pp), which has bath and shower facilities; bring a sleeping bag and mosquito netting. You can buy groceries at a small store immediately below the ranger station at Las Pailas.

Getting There

To the Santa María Ranger Station: The road begins in the Barrio Victoria suburb of Liberia (a sign on Hwy. 1 on the south side of Liberia points the way to Sector Santa María), where Avenida 6 leads east 25 kilometers (16 miles) past the ranger station entrance to the hamlets of San Jorge and Colonia Blanca (which can also be reached by a dirt road from Guayabo, north of Bagaces). The road is deeply rutted, and muddy in wet season; a

4WD vehicle is recommended. Santa María is linked to Las Pailas by a six-kilometer (4-mile) trail and by a dirt road that passes through private property ($1.50 toll).

To the Las Pailas Ranger Station: Las Pailas is reached off the Pan-American Highway via a dirt road that begins about six kilometers (4 miles) north of Liberia. The road leads past the village of Curubandé (at 10 kilometers/6 miles) to the gates of Hacienda Guachipelín cattle ranch (the gates are open during daylight hours; $1.50 toll, reimbursed if you stay here). The road leads three kilometers (2 miles) to Hacienda Lodge Guachipelín and, beyond, to Las Pailas Ranger Station. A bus departs Liberia for Curubandé and Hacienda Lodge Guachipelín at 4:15am, 12:45pm, and 4:15pm daily.

Lodges arrange transfers, and the Hotel Guanacaste in Liberia has transfers ($7 pp each way, minimum 3 people) at 7am and 4pm daily. A taxi from Liberia will cost about $30-40 each way.

AROUND RINCÓN DE LA VIEJA

Several nature lodges on the lower slopes of Rincón de la Vieja double as activity centers and accept day visitors.

Hacienda Lodge Guachipelín (tel. 506/2690-2900, www.guachipelin.com), a 100-year-old working cattle ranch east of Curubandé, 18 kilometers (11 miles) from Highway 1, has more than 1,000 hectares (2,400 acres) of terrain from dry forest to open savanna, plus a 1,200-hectare (2,965-acre) tree-reforestation project. Activities include guided horseback rides (adults $62, children $52), waterfall rappelling (adults $55, students $45, children $35), river tubing (adults $55, children $50, including horseback ride), plus the **Cañón Canopy Tour** (adults $50, students $40, children $30), where you can whiz across a canyon and between treetops from 10 platforms. A one-day Adventure Pass (adults $85, students $80, children $75) lets you partake in all the fun. Afterward you'll want to soothe away any aches at its **Simbiosis**

Volcanic Mud Springs & Spa (www.simbi-osis-spa.com), close to the Las Pailas Ranger Station. The lodge also has frogs, snakes, and butterfly exhibits (extra cost).

Buena Vista Mountain Lodge & Adventure Center (tel. 506/2690-1414, www.buenavistalodgecr.com), a 1,600-hectare (3,950-acre) ranch nestling high on the north-west flank of the mountain, offers guided hikes and horseback trips ($40-45), plus an 11-platform zip-line canopy tour ($40), an aerial trail with 17 hanging bridges ($25), and a 420-meter (1,380-foot) waterslide—like a toboggan run—ending with a plunge into a pool ($15). It also has frogs, snakes, and butterfly exhibits ($10), plus the deluxe **Tizate Wellness Garden Hot Springs & Spa,** with five hot spring pools linked by boardwalks and a sumptuous massage and treatment center. It's reached via the hamlet of Cañas Dulces, four kilometers (2.5 miles) east of Highway 1: The turnoff is 11 kilometers (7 miles) north of Liberia (don't mistake this for Cañas, farther south on Hwy. 1). Beyond Cañas Dulces, the road turns to dirt and climbs uphill 13 kilometers (8 miles) to Buena Vista.

One kilometer (0.6 miles) below Buena Vista Lodge, a side road leads three kilometers (2 miles) to **Hotel Borinquen Mountain Resort & Spa** (tel. 506/2690-1900, www.borinquenresort.com), an upscale moun-tain resort built around bubbling *pilas* (mud ponds) that feed the lovely **Amhra Sidae Spa,** which specializes in thermal treatments, including full-body mineral mud masks ($65). It has plunge pools (one hot, one tepid, one cold) and a beautiful landscaped swimming pool with a whirlpool tub. Borinquen also of-fers guided hiking (adults $20, children $10), horseback riding, a waterfall ride (by ATV $40, by horse $35), and a canopy adventure (adults $55, children $27.50). It is surrounded by primary forest accessed by trails (pass on the lame "ecotour"). One-day packages are available.

Buses depart Liberia daily for Cañas Dulces at 5:30am, noon, and 5:30pm daily, but you'll need a Jeep taxi to reach the two activity center-resorts.

Accommodations and Food

To escape the tour groups that often de-scend on the activity centers, my lodging of choice is the bargain-priced Belgian-run ★ **Aroma de Campo** (tel. 506/2665-0008, www.aromadecampo.com, $49 s, $67.50 d, in-cluding breakfast), a secluded hacienda-style

Horses get a daily hose-down at Hacienda Lodge Guachipelín.

bed-and-breakfast with four simple yet exquisitely romantic rooms, each in a rich, vibrant color scheme (avocado green, eggplant, papaya, or salmon), with gauzy drapes over the beds. It exudes a perfect combination of traditional architecture and a contemporary European aesthetic, such as glazed concrete floors. Quality meals are served family-style on the open-air patio with hammocks, Adirondack chairs, and lovely views. Wi-Fi is included.

Once merely a working cattle ranch, **Hacienda Lodge Guachipelín** (tel. 506/2666-8075, U.S./Canada tel. 877-998-7873, www.guachipelin.com, $81-173 s, $99-173 d year-round) has evolved into an eco-lodge that specializes in adventure tours. It boasts a gracious lobby with exquisite wrought-iron sofas, Internet access, and a bar overlooking a kidney-shaped pool under shade trees. The 34 older bedrooms are small and simply appointed but have fans and wide verandas; 18 newer units are slightly more elegant. Four junior suites in the old *casona* overlook the corral, where you can watch cattle and horses being worked. The stone and timber bar-restaurant (6am-10pm daily) at the entrance to the hacienda is open to the public and serves buffet dinners to the accompaniment of marimba players.

With a loftier perch than Hacienda Lodge Guachipelín, yet in a similar vein, the **Buena Vista Mountain Lodge & Adventure Center** (tel. 506/2665-7759, www.buenavistalodgecr.com, $65-80 s, $70-100 d year-round) has 77 rooms and rustic yet delightful cabins of stone and rough timbers, with pewter-washed floors and verandas looking down over lush lawns and, in some, a lake. You can admire the setting while soaking in a natural steam bath ringed by volcanic stone, and there's a bamboo sauna. It provides transfers from Cañas Dulces. A rustic restaurant serves buffet meals. You can camp for $10.

The upscale **Hotel Borinquen Mountain Resort & Spa** (tel. 506/2690-1900, www.borinquenresort.com, low season from $144 s, $159 d, high season from $166 s, $185 d), in colonial hacienda style, offers 39 spacious air-conditioned rooms (including graciously appointed deluxe rooms and junior suites) in single and duplex red-tile-roofed villas and bungalows spaced apart on the grassy hills. They're well lit and are graced by handmade furnishings, including wrought-iron candelabras and rustic antiques (take your pick of decor: pre-Columbian or Spanish colonial). Guests move around on electric golf carts. Facilities include a tennis court, a beauty salon, a gym, a spa, and a swimming pool with a swim-up bar.

The Far North

★ SANTA ROSA NATIONAL PARK

Founded in 1972, **Parque Nacional Santa Rosa** (www.sinac.go.cr) was the country's first national park. The 49,515-hectare (122,354-acre) park covers much of the Santa Elena peninsula and is part of a mosaic of ecologically interdependent parks and reserves—the 110,000-hectare (272,000-acre) Área de Conservación Guanacaste. Parque Nacional Santa Rosa is most famous for Hacienda Santa Rosa—better known as La Casona—the nation's most cherished historic monument. It was here in 1856 that the mercenary army of American adventurer William Walker was defeated by a ragamuffin army of Costa Rican volunteers.

The park is a mosaic of 10 distinct habitats, including mangrove swamp, savanna, and oak forest, which attract more than 250 bird species and 115 mammal species (half of them bats, including two vampire species), among them relatively easily seen animals such as white-tailed deer; coatimundis; howler, spider, and white-faced monkeys; and anteaters. In the wet season, the land is as green as emeralds, and the wildlife disperses. In dry season, however, wildlife congregates at watering holes and is easily spotted. Jaguars, margays, ocelots, pumas, and jaguarundis are here but are seldom seen. Santa Rosa is a vitally important nesting site for olive ridleys and other turtle species.

The park is divided into two sections: the more important and accessible Santa Rosa Sector to the south (the entrance is at Km. 269 on Hwy. 1, about 37 kilometers/23 miles north of Liberia) and the Murciélago Sector (the turnoff from Hwy. 1 is 10 kilometers/6 miles farther north, via Cuajiniquil), separated by a swath of privately owned land.

Santa Rosa Sector

From the entrance gate, the paved road leads six kilometers (4 miles) to **La Casona,** a magnificent colonial homestead (actually, it's a replica, rebuilt in 2001 after arsonists burned down the original) overlooking a stone corral where the battle with William Walker was fought. The fire destroyed the antique furnishings and collection of photos, illustrations, carbines, and other military paraphernalia commemorating the battle of March 20, 1856. Battles were also fought here during the 1919 Sapoá Revolution and in 1955. The garden contains rocks with petroglyphs.

The 1.5-kilometer (1-mile) **Naked Indian loop trail** begins just before La Casona and leads through dry forest with streams, waterfalls, and gumbo-limbo trees whose peeling red bark earned them the nickname "naked Indian trees." **Los Patos trail** has watering holes and is one of the best trails for spotting mammals.

The paved road ends just beyond the administration area, near La Casona. From here, a rugged dirt road drops steeply to **Playa Naranjo,** 13 kilometers (8 miles). A 4WD vehicle with high ground clearance is essential, but passage is never guaranteed, not least because the Río Nisperal can be impassable in wet season (the beach is usually off-limits

Aug.-Nov.). Park officials sometimes close the road and will charge you a fee if you have to be hauled out. Playa Naranjo is a beautiful kilometers-long pale-gray-sand beach that is legendary in surfing lore for its steep, powerful tubular waves and for **Witch's Rock,** rising like a sentinel out of the water. The beach is bounded by craggy headlands and frequently visited by monkeys, iguanas, and other wildlife. Crocodiles lurk in mangrove swamps at the southern end of the beach. At night, plankton light up with a brilliant phosphorescence as you walk the drying sand in the wake of high tide.

The deserted white-sand **Playa Nancite,** about one hour's hike over a headland from Estero Real, is renowned as a site for *arribadas,* the mass nestings of olive ridley turtles. More than 75,000 turtles will gather out at sea and come ashore over the space of a few days, with the possibility of up to 10,000 of them on the beach at any one time in September and October. You can usually see solitary turtles at other times August through December. Playa Nancite is a research site; access is restricted and permits are required, although anyone can get one from the ranger station or at the **Dry Tropical Forest Investigation Center** (Centro de los Investigaciones, tel. 506/2666-5051, ext. 233), next to the administrative center, which undertakes biological research. It is not open to visitors.

Playa Potrero Grande, north of Nancite, and other beaches on the central Santa Elena peninsula offer some of the best surf in the country. The makers of *Endless Summer II,* the sequel to the classic surfing movie, captured the Potrero Grande break on film perfectly. You can hire a boat at any of the fishing villages in the Golfo Santa Elena to take you to Potrero Grande or **Islas Murciélagos** (Bat Islands), off Cabo Santa Elena, the westernmost point of the peninsula. The islands are a renowned scuba site for advanced divers.

Murciélago Sector

The entrance to the Murciélago Sector of Parque Nacional Santa Rosa is 15 kilometers

Santa Rosa and Guanacaste National Parks

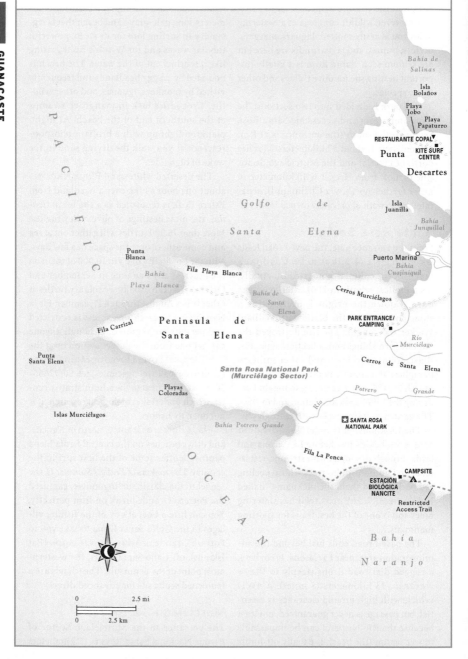

Bahía de
Salinas

Isla
Bolaños

Playa
Jobo

Playa
Papaturro

RESTAURANTE COPAL

Punta KITE SURF
CENTER

Descartes

Golfo   de

Isla
Juanilla

Bahía
Junquillal

Santa   Elena

Punta
Blanca

Puerto Marina

Bahía
Cuajiniquil

Bahía   Fila Playa Blanca
Playa Blanca

Bahía de
Santa
Elena

Cerros Murciélagos

PARK ENTRANCE/
CAMPING

Fila Carrizal

Peninsula   de
Santa   Elena

Río
Murciélago

Cerros   de Santa Elena

Punta
Santa Elena

Santa Rosa National Park
(Murciélago Sector)

Playas
Coloradas

Potrero   Grande

Islas Murciélagos

Bahía Potrero Grande

SANTA ROSA
NATIONAL PARK

Fila La Penca

CAMPSITE

ESTACIÓN
BIOLÓGICA
NANCITE

Restricted
Access Trail

Bahía

Naranjo

0   2.5 mi

0   2.5 km

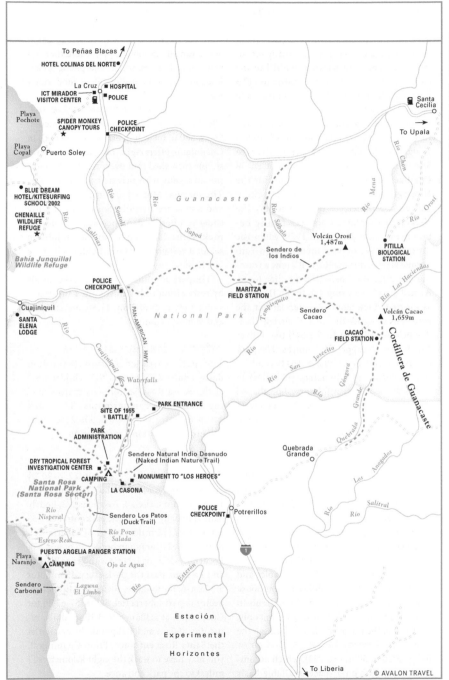

To Peñas Blacas
HOTEL COLINAS DEL NORTE

La Cruz
ICT MIRADOR
VISITOR CENTER
HOSPITAL
POLICE

Santa
Cecilia

Playa
Pochote
SPIDER MONKEY
CANOPY TOURS
POLICE
CHECKPOINT

To Upala

Playa
Copal
Puerto Soley

Rio Chan

BLUE DREAM
HOTEL/KITESURFING
SCHOOL 2002

Guanacaste

Rio

Rio

Rio Sabalo

Rio Mena

Rio Orosi

Rio

CHENAILLE
WILDLIFE
REFUGE

Rio

Sapoá

Volcán Orosí
1,487m

Rio Santoli

Bahía Junquillal
Wildlife Refuge

Salinas

Sendero de
los Indios

PITILLA
BIOLOGICAL
STATION

POLICE
CHECKPOINT

MARITZA
FIELD STATION

Rio Las Haciendas

Cuajiniquil

SANTA
ELENA
LODGE

National Park

Tempisquito

Sendero
Cacao

Volcán Cacao
1,659m

Rio

CACAO
FIELD STATION

PAN-AMERICAN HWY

Rio

Rio San Josecito

Gingora

Cordillera de Guanacaste

Cuajiniquil

Waterfalls

Rio

Rio

Grande

SITE OF 1955
BATTLE

PARK ENTRANCE

Quebrada

PARK
ADMINISTRATION

Sendero Natural Indio Desnudo
(Naked Indian Nature Trail)

Quebrada
Grande

Los Angulos

DRY TROPICAL FOREST
INVESTIGATION CENTER

CAMPING

MONUMENT TO "LOS HEROES"

Santa Rosa
National Park
(Santa Rosa Sector)

LA CASONA

Rio
Nisperal

Sendero Los Patos
(Duck Trail)

POLICE
CHECKPOINT
Potrerillos

Rio Salitral

Rio

Estero Real

Río Poza
Salada

Playa
Naranjo
PUESTO ARGELIA RANGER STATION
CAMPING

Ojo de Agua

Estero

Sendero
Carbonal
Laguna
El Limbo

Rio

Estación
Experimental
Horizontes

To Liberia

© AVALON TRAVEL

(9.5 miles) west of Highway 1, and 10 kilometers (6 miles) north of the Santa Rosa Sector park entrance (there's a police checkpoint at the turnoff; have your passport ready for inspection). The road winds downhill to the hamlet of Cuajiniquil, tucked 500 meters (0.3 miles) south of the road, which continues to Bahía Cuajiniquil.

You arrive at a Y-fork in Cuajiniquil; the road to Murciélago, eight kilometers (5 miles) along, is to the left. There are three rivers to ford en route. You'll pass the old U.S. Central Intelligence Agency training camp for the Nicaraguan Contras on the right. The site—Hacienda Murciélago—was owned by the Nicaraguan dictator Somoza's family before being expropriated in 1979, when the Murciélago Sector was incorporated into Parque Nacional Santa Rosa. It's now a training camp for the Costa Rican police force. Armed guards may stop you for an ID check as you pass. A few hundred meters farther, the road runs alongside the "secret" airstrip (hidden behind tall grass to the left) that Oliver North built to supply the Contras. The park entrance is 500 meters (0.3 miles) beyond.

It's another 16 kilometers (10 miles) to Playa Blanca, a beautiful horseshoe-shaped white-sand beach about five kilometers (3 miles) wide and enjoyed only by pelicans and frigate birds. The road ends here.

Accommodations and Food

The Santa Rosa Sector has two public campsites. La Casona campsite ($2 pp), 400 meters (0.25 miles) west of the administrative center, is shaded by *guanacaste* trees and has barbecue pits, picnic tables, and restrooms. It can get muddy here in the wet season. The shady Argelia campsite at Playa Naranjo has sites with fire pits and picnic tables and benches. It has showers, sinks, and outhouse toilets, but no water. The campsite at the north end of Playa Nancite is for use by permit only, obtained at the ranger station or through the Dry Tropical Forest Investigation Center (tel. 506/2666-5051, ext. 233), which accommodates guests on a space-available basis

(adults $15, scientists $10, students and assistants $6). Reservations are recommended.

In the Murciélago Sector, you can camp at the ranger station ($2 pp), where there's a restroom, showers, water, and picnic tables. Raccoons abound and scavenge food; don't feed them.

The rustic Santa Elena Lodge (tel. 506/2679-1038, www.santaelenalodge.com, $60 s, $80 d, including breakfast and tax), in Cuajiniquil, offers eight spacious and cozy yet simply furnished (but overpriced) air-conditioned rooms with private hot-water baths. The owners, Manuel, a former fisherman, and Sonia, are friendly. Sonia will proudly show you her garden enclosed by volcanic rock walls. The couple runs an adjoining seafood restaurant. Manuel will gladly take you fishing.

The park administration area serves meals by reservation only (minimum 2 hours advance notice, 6am-7am, 11:30am-12:30pm, and 5pm-6pm daily).

Information and Services

The park entrance station (8am-4pm daily, adults $10, surfers $15, children $1) at the Santa Rosa Sector sells maps showing trails and campgrounds. The park administration office (tel. 506/2666-5051) can provide additional information.

Getting There

Transportes Deldú (tel. 506/2256-9072) buses depart San José for La Cruz and Peñas Blancas from Calle 20, Avenidas 1/3, hourly 3am-7pm daily, passing the park entrance—35 kilometers (22 miles) north of Liberia—en route to the Nicaraguan border (6 hours, $5). Local buses linking Liberia with Peñas Blancas and La Cruz pass the park every 45 minutes 5:30am-6:30pm daily. Buses to Murciélago Sector depart Liberia (tel. 506/8357-6769) for Cuajiniquil at 5:30am and 3:30pm daily, returning at 7am and 4:30pm daily; catch it at the Santa Rosa entrance. From Cuajiniquil, you may have to walk the eight kilometers (5 miles) to the park entrance.

GUANACASTE NATIONAL PARK

Little-visited Parque Nacional Guanacaste (tel. 506/2666-7718 or 506/2666-5051, Sector Pocosol tel. 506/2661-8150, www.sinac.go.cr, by reservation only, $10) protects more than 84,000 hectares (208,000 acres) of savanna, dry forest, rainforest, and cloud forests extending east from Highway 1 to the top of Volcán Cacao at 1,659 meters (5,443 feet). The park is contiguous with Parque Nacional Santa Rosa to the west and protects the migratory routes of myriad creatures, many of which move seasonally between the lowlands and the steep slopes of Volcán Cacao and the dramatically conical yet dormant Volcán Orosi (1,487 meters/4,879 feet), whose rain-drenched eastern slopes contrast sharply with the dry plains.

It is one of the most closely monitored parks scientifically, with three permanent biological stations. The Pitilla Biological Station is at 600 meters (1,970 feet) elevation on the northeast side of Cacao amid the lush rain-soaked forest. It's a nine-kilometer (5.5-mile) drive via Esperanza on a rough dirt road from Santa Cecilia, 28 kilometers (17 miles) east of Highway 1. A 4WD vehicle is essential. Cacao Field Station, also called Mengo, sits at the edge of a cloud forest at 1,100 meters (3,600 feet) on the southwestern slope of Volcán Cacao. You can get there by hiking or taking a horse 10 kilometers (6 miles) along a rough dirt trail from Quebrada Grande; the turnoff from Highway 1 is at Potrerillos, nine kilometers (5.5 miles) south of the Parque Nacional Santa Rosa turnoff. You'll see a sign for the station 500 meters (0.3 miles) beyond Dos Ríos, which is 11 kilometers (7 miles) beyond Quebrada Grande. The road—paved for the first four kilometers (2.5 miles)—deteriorates gradually. With a 4WD vehicle you can make it to within 300 meters (1,000 feet) of the station in dry season, with permission; in wet season you'll need to park at Gongora, about five kilometers (3 miles) before Cacao, and proceed on foot or horseback.

Maritza Field Station is farther north, at about 650 meters (2,130 feet) elevation on the western side of the saddle between the Cacao and Orosi volcanoes. You get there from Highway 1 via a 15-kilometer (9.5-mile) dirt road to the right at the Cuajiniquil crossroads. There are barbed-wire gates; simply close them behind you. A 4WD vehicle is essential in wet season. The station has a research laboratory. From here you can hike to Cacao Field Station. Another trail leads to El Pedregal, on the western slope of Volcán Orosi, where almost 100 petroglyphs representing a pantheon of chiseled supernatural beings lie partly buried in the luxurious undergrowth.

Accommodations

You can camp at any of the field stations ($2 per day), which also provide Spartan dormitory accommodations on a space-available basis; for reservations, contact the park headquarters in Parque Nacional Santa Rosa, which can also arrange transportation. Cacao Field Station has a lodge with five rustic dormitories for up to 30 people. It has water, but no towels or electricity. Maritza Field Station is less rustic and has beds for 32 people, with shared baths, water, electricity, and a dining hall. The Pitilla Biological Station has accommodations for 20 people, with electricity, water, and basic meals. Students and researchers get priority. Rates for all are $15 for adult visitors, $10 for scientists, and $6 for students and assistants.

LA CRUZ AND VICINITY

La Cruz, gateway to Nicaragua, 19 kilometers (12 miles) north, is dramatically situated atop an escarpment east of Bahía de Salinas. A Costa Rican Tourist Board-run mirador (lookout) 100 meters (330 feet) west of the town plaza offers a spectacular view over the bay.

Bahía Salinas

From the mirador, a paved road drops to the flask-shaped Bahía Salinas, a windsurfing and kiteboarding mecca ringed by beaches backed by scrub-covered plains lined with salt pans

Restoring the Dry Forest

Parque Nacional Guanacaste includes large expanses of eroded pasture that were once covered with native dry forest, which at the time of the Spaniards' colonization carpeted a greater area of Mesoamerica than did rainforests. It was also more vulnerable to encroaching civilization. After 400 years of burning, only 2 percent of Central America's dry forest remained. Fires, set to clear pasture, often become free-running blazes that sweep across the landscape. If the fires can be quelled, trees can take root again.

For four decades, American biologist Daniel Janzen has led an attempt to restore Costa Rica's vanished dry forest to nearly 60,000 hectares (148,000 acres) of ranchland around a remnant 10,000-hectare (24,700-acre) nucleus. Janzen, a professor of ecology at the University of Pennsylvania, has spent six months of every year for more than 40 years studying the intricate relationships between animals and plants in Guanacaste.

A key to success is to nurture a conservation ethic among the surrounding communities. Education for grade-school children is viewed as part of the ongoing management of the park; all fourth-, fifth-, and sixth-grade children in the region get an intense course in basic biology. Many of the farmers who formerly ranched land are being retrained as park guards, research assistants, and guides.

Another 2,400-hectare (5,930-acre) project is centered on Reserva Biológica Lomas Barbudal in southern Guanacaste. Lomas Barbudal is one of the few remaining Pacific coast forests favored by the endangered scarlet macaw, which has a penchant for the seeds of the sandbox tree (the Spanish found the seed's hard casing perfect for storing sand, which was sprinkled on documents to absorb wet ink; hence its name).

and mangroves that attract wading birds and crocodiles. The beaches are of white sand fading to brown-gray along the shore of **Punta Descartes,** separating the bay from Bahía Junquillal to the south. High winds blow almost nonstop December-April, making this a prime spot for windsurfing.

The road, unpaved and in horrendous shape, leads past the hamlet of **Puerto Soley,** where the road splits. The right fork leads via **Playa Papaturro** to **Jobo,** a fishing village at the tip of Punta Descartes. Turn right in Jobo for **Playa Jobo** and **Playa la Coyotera.** The left fork leads to Bahía Junquillal; a 4WD vehicle is essential (this route was impassable during my last rainy-season visit due to mud and a washed-out bridge). En route, you'll pass **Refugio de Vida Silvestre Chenailles,** a private wildlife refuge not currently open to the public.

Refugio Nacional de Vida Silvestre Isla Bolaños (Bolaños Island National Wildlife Refuge) protects one of only four nesting sites in Costa Rica for the brown pelican, and the only known nesting site for the American oystercatcher. Frigate birds also nest on the rocky crag, about 500 meters (0.3 miles) east of Punta Descartes, during the January-March mating season. Visitors are not allowed to set foot on the island, but you can hire a boat and a guide in Puerto Soley or Jobo to take you within 50 meters (165 feet).

Recreation

Eco-Wind (tel. 506/2235-8810, www.ecoplaya. com, high season only) surf center at Eco-Playa Resort, at Playa Papaturro, and the **Kite Surf Center** (Blue Dream Hotel & Spa, tel. 506/8826-5221, www.bluedreamhotel.com) rent boards and offer classes and courses in windsurfing.

Ashore, adrenaline junkies can get their highs at **Spider Monkey Canopy Tour** (tel. 506/2679-8227), with its 11-cable zip line, on the road to Bahía Solanos.

Accommodations and Food

My favorite hostelry is **Amalia's Inn** (tel./fax 506/2679-9618, $25 pp), 100 meters (330 feet) south of the plaza. This charming place is operated by a friendly Tica and boasts a fabulous cliff-top perch with views over Bahía Salinas. Its eight rooms are large and cool, with tile floors, leather sofas, and striking paintings by the owner's late father, Lester Bounds. All have private baths. A pool is handy for cooling off, though the inn's setting is breezy enough. Breakfast and picnics are prepared on request.

The modern two-story **Blue Dream Hotel** (tel. 506/8826-5221, www.bluedream-hotel.com, Nov.-Sept., from $25 s, $35 d), at Playa Papaturro, specializes in windsurfing and has nine rooms, including a budget dorm room ($12 pp), with terra-cotta floors and sliding glass doors to terraces with views, plus four larger wooden rooms for three people. The restaurant serves Italian fare, including pizza, and jams in locals for postprandial pleasures such as videos and live music under the stars. Its room rates are inanely complicated, varying almost monthly. It closes for October.

Information and Services

There's a bank opposite the gas station on Highway 1 as you enter La Cruz. The **police** **station** (tel. 506/2679-9117), **Red Cross** (tel. 506/2679-9146), and **medical clinic** (tel. 506/2679-9116) are here too. There's an Internet café next to Amalia's Inn.

Getting There

Transportes Deldú (tel. 506/2256-9072) buses depart San José for La Cruz and Peñas Blancas from Calle 20, Avenidas 1/3, hourly 3am-7pm daily. Local buses depart Liberia for Peñas Blancas via La Cruz every 45 minutes 5:30am-6:30pm daily. You can buy bus tickets from the *pulpería* (tel. 506/2679-9108) next to the bus station. For a taxi, call **Taxi La Cruz** (tel. 506/2679-9112).

Buses (tel. 506/2659-8278) depart La Cruz five times daily for Puerto Soley and Jobo. A taxi from La Cruz will cost about $3 one-way to Puerto Soley, $8 to Jobo.

PEÑAS BLANCAS: CROSSING INTO NICARAGUA

Peñas Blancas, 19 kilometers (12 miles) north of La Cruz, is the border post for Nicaragua. Be careful driving the Pan-American Highway, which hereabouts is dangerously potholed and chockablock with articulated

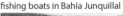
fishing boats in Bahía Junquillal

trucks hurtling along. Steel yourself for a very lengthy and frustrating border-crossing process.

The bus terminal contains the **Oficina de Migración** (immigration office, tel. 506/2679-9025), a bank, a restaurant, and the **Costa Rican Tourism Institute** (ICT, tel. 506/2677-0138). Change money before crossing into Nicaragua (you get a better exchange rate on the Costa Rican side).

Transportes Deldú (tel. 506/2256-9072) buses depart San José for La Cruz and Peñas Blancas from Calle 20, Avenidas 1/3, hourly 3am-7pm daily. Local buses depart Liberia for Peñas Blancas via La Cruz every 45 minutes 5:30am-6:30pm daily.

Bahía Salinas

MAP SYMBOLS

═══	Expressway	○	City/Town	✈	Airport	⚓	Golf Course
───	Primary Road	◉	State Capital	✈	Airfield	🅿	Parking Area
───	Secondary Road	⊛	National Capital	▲	Mountain	⛟	Archaeological Site
······	Unpaved Road	★	Point of Interest	✛	Unique Natural Feature	⛪	Church
───	Feature Trail	●	Accommodation		Waterfall	⛽	Gas Station
------	Other Trail	▼	Restaurant/Bar	▲	Park		Glacier
··········	Ferry	■	Other Location	⬟	Trailhead		Mangrove
───	Pedestrian Walkway	Δ	Campground	⛷	Skiing Area		Reef
⊞⊞⊞	Stairs						Swamp

CONVERSION TABLES

°C = (°F – 32) / 1.8
°F = (°C x 1.8) + 32
1 inch = 2.54 centimeters (cm)
1 foot = 0.304 meters (m)
1 yard = 0.914 meters
1 mile = 1.6093 kilometers (km)
1 km = 0.6214 miles
1 fathom = 1.8288 m
1 chain = 20.1168 m
1 furlong = 201.168 m
1 acre = 0.4047 hectares
1 sq km = 100 hectares
1 sq mile = 2.59 square km
1 ounce = 28.35 grams
1 pound = 0.4536 kilograms
1 short ton = 0.90718 metric ton
1 short ton = 2,000 pounds
1 long ton = 1.016 metric tons
1 long ton = 2,240 pounds
1 metric ton = 1,000 kilograms
1 quart = 0.94635 liters
1 US gallon = 3.7854 liters
1 Imperial gallon = 4.5459 liters
1 nautical mile = 1.852 km

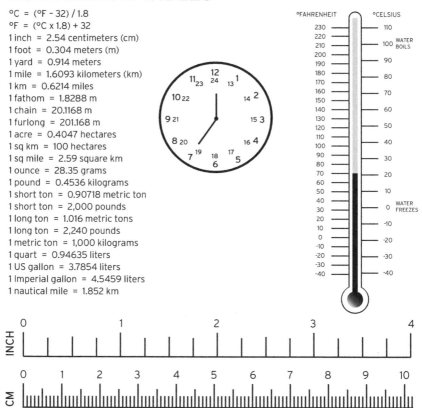

MOON SPOTLIGHT ARENAL &
MONTEVERDE
Avalon Travel
a member of the Perseus Books Group
1700 Fourth Street
Berkeley, CA 94710, USA
www.moon.com

Editor: Nikki Ioakimedes
Series Manager: Kathryn Ettinger
Copy Editor: Christopher Church
Graphics and Production Coordinator:
   Lucie Ericksen
Map Editor: Mike Morgenfeld
Cartographer: Brian Shotwell

ISBN-13: 978-1-63121-241-3

Front cover photo: Arenal Volcano © Steffen
   Foerster | Dreamstime.com
Title page photo: Tortuguero Lagoon and
   Tortuguero village © Christopher P. Baker
All interior photos: © Christopher P. Baker

Printed in the United States

About the Author

Christopher P. Baker

Christopher P. Baker was born and raised in Yorkshire, England. He received a bachelors degree in geography from University College, London, and masters degrees in Latin American studies from Liverpool University and in education from the Institute of Education, London University.

He began his writing career in 1978 as a contributing editor on Latin America for *Land & Liberty*, a London-based political journal. In 1980, he received a Scripps-Howard Foundation Scholarship in Journalism to attend the University of California, Berkeley.

Since 1983, Christopher, the 2008 Lowell Thomas Travel Journalist of the Year, has made his living as a professional travel writer, photographer, lecturer, and tour guide. He specializes in Cuba and Costa Rica, about which he has written six books each, including *Moon Cuba* and his most recent coffee-table book, *Enchanting Costa Rica*. He is also the author of the *Costa Rica Pura Vida!* travel app. He has contributed to more than 150 publications worldwide, including CNN Travel, *National Geographic Traveler, Robb Report,* and *The Los Angeles Times.* He is a Getty Images and *National Geographic* contributing photographer.

Christopher has been profiled in *USA Today*, appears frequently on radio and television talk shows and as a guest-lecturer aboard cruise ships, and has spoken at the National Press Club, World Affairs Council, and on *National Geographic Live.* He is a *National Geographic* Resident Expert and leads tours of Costa Rica, Panama, Colombia, and Cuba for *National Geographic* Expeditions, as well as group motorcycle tours of these destinations for MotoDiscovery and Motolombia.

Christopher promotes himself through his website: www.christopherpbaker.com.

CPSIA information can be obtained at www.ICGtesting.com
Printed in the USA
LVOW01s0249250915

455610LV00001B/1/P